THE
INTERNATIONAL BOOK
OF
SACRED SONG

THE INTERNATIONAL BOOK OF SACRED SONG

WALTER EHRET
MELINDA EDWARDS
GEORGE K. EVANS

Woodcuts by Fritz Kredel

PRENTICE-HALL, INC., Englewood Cliffs, N.J. 07632

The International Book of Sacred Song
by Walter Ehret, Melinda Edwards and
George K. Evans
© 1969 by Prentice-Hall, Inc.

Printed in the United States of America

Prentice-Hall International, Inc., London
Prentice-Hall of Australia, Pty. Ltd., Sydney
Prentice-Hall of Canada, Ltd., Toronto
Prentice-Hall of India Private Ltd., New Delhi
Prentice-Hall of Japan, Inc., Tokyo
Prentice-Hall of Southeast Asia Pt. Ltd., Singapore
Whitehall Books Limited, Wellington, New Zealand

10 9 8 7 6 5 4 3 2 1

ISBN 0-13-471649-3 (PBK)

Introduction

"*Sing unto the Lord a new song; sing unto the Lord all the earth.*" The beginning of Psalm 96 expresses a thought that men have heeded for centuries. Because song is such a personal form of expression, vocal music is an integral part of almost all worship services. For thousands of years, thousands of churches have rung with song.

Perhaps the most common type of religious music performed in services today is the hymn. St. Augustine said that hymns are praises to God with singing. A hymn is a religious poem which is set to music in stanza form; that is, the same tune is sung to each verse of the poem. There are four basic kinds of hymns, only one of which is not closely connected with the Biblical Book of Psalms.

(1) Original Hebrew psalms, or psalms with a literal Latin or vernacular translation.

(2) Metrical versions of psalms.

(3) Free paraphrases of the psalms.

(4) Original poems based on other scriptural texts or the authors' religious experiences or concepts.

All early peoples, including pagan civilizations, have sung hymns. The songs of the ancient Hebrews as found in the Bible can be considered the ancestors of Christian hymnody. The first recorded history of Hebrew music appears in Genesis 4:21, and dates from about 3875 B.C. It identifies Jubal, a lineal descendant of Cain, as the "father of all such as handle the harp and organ." The first recorded *hymn* in the Bible is credited to Moses in Exodus 15:1-18 Music has had a lengthy and honorable tradition among the Jews and it was in the Holy Land, where synagogue music began more than two thousand years ago, that Christian music had its beginning.

The Davidic tradition is the oldest in Jewish music. A thousand years before Christ, David, a musician and principal author of the Psalms, appointed the Levites to provide music for temple services. This ancient temple music was probably elaborate, being performed by a large choir and an orchestra of instruments such as the *hasosra chatzotzra*, a silver trumpet; the *magrepha*, a pipe organ; the *tziltzal*, cymbals; the *nevel*, a large harp; the *kinnor*, a lyre; and the *shofar*, a ram's horn. (The latter, a signaling instrument, still survives and is used in Jewish rites today.) The congregation sang the daily psalm and the Scriptures were intoned in a sing-song voice. This process, called cantillation, continued until the destruction of the Temple of Jerusalem by the Emperor Titus in A.D. 70.

By the nineteenth century, European synagogue music was being influenced by men like Salomon Sulzer, who was close to Franz Schubert; Louis Lewandowski, who was himself influenced by the style of Mendelssohn's oratorios; Samuel Naumbourg, influenced by the Paris grand opera style Hirsch Weintraub, who wrote in the manner of Schumann and Loewe: Edward Birnbaum, who attempted to imitate Wagner; Baruch Schorr, who was familiar with the Russian music of Glinka and Moussorgsky.

In nineteenth-century America, Reform Judaism brought a mixture of many elements to form the musical services: old tunes were used with new texts; new settings were supplied for traditional Hebrew melodies; Jewish and American folk tunes as well as some tunes borrowed from Protestant hymnody were adapted.

In the twentieth century, scholars like A. W. Binder and A. Z. Idelsohn, and serious composers such as Ernest Bloch, Leonard Bernstein, Arnold Schönberg, and Darius Milhaud have contributed to Jewish service music as we know it today.

The true foundation of Christian hymnody also lies in the Book of Psalms, the hymnbook of the Hebrews, and an immortal collection of religious poetry which has been a continual source of inspiration to men of all faiths. Another early Biblical source of Christian hymnody was the New Testament canticles, which have provided many texts for the Roman Catholic liturgy. A canticle is a biblical song not occurring in the Book of Psalms. Often they were songs of Christian experience, sung by the early Christians as supplements to the Psalms. They have since been set to music by composers of all periods. The *Magnificat* was Mary's song of praise to God after the angel Gabriel's visitation. The *Benedictus* was Zachariah's song after the birth of his son. *Gloria in Excelis* was sung by the angels to the shepherds on Christmas night. *Nunc Dimittis* was Simeon's song upon seeing Jesus, the one who would redeem Israel, with Joseph and Mary in the temple.

Turning from Biblical sources, we find that many of the earliest hymn writers were Greeks. Men such as Clement of Alexandria (*c.* 150- *c.* 215), Andrew of Crete (660-740), John of Damascus (*c.* 675-749), Stephen the Sabiate (725-794), and St. Anatolius (*d.* 458) found that hymns were a means of teaching, of persuasion to be converted, and they were effective as a weapon against heresy.

Unhappily, no Latin hymns of the period before the fourth century have been found. The ancient Christian church used either Greek or Latin depending upon location, but by the fourth century all the Western countries had been romanized, and therefore Latin was used in the services. One of the great names in early church history was St. Ambrose (333-397). The Bishop of Milan and the "father of Western church song," Ambrose wrote metrical hymns and undertook to codify Western church music, a task which Pope Gregory the Great (540-604) finished some centuries later. Other early Christian poets whose hymns found their way into the liturgy were Aurelius Prudentius (348-410?) and Venantius Fortunatus (*c.* 540-*c.* 600).

During the Dark Ages and the later medieval period, many hymns came from the monasteries or from itinerant orders such as the Franciscans, led by St. Francis of Assisi, who gave up wealth to embrace poverty and preach to the poor. Hymns by Peter Abélard (1079-1142), Bernard of Cluny (12th century), and Bernard of Clairvaux (1090-1153) issued forth from their cloister retreats. A leader at the St. Gall Monastery, Nother Balbulus (840-912), was responsible for the development of what is called the sequence. This was a melismatic (many notes sung to one syllable) song, originally sung to the word "alleluia." Nother wrote other words to go with sequence music for almost all of the holy days in the church year.

In 1517 an extremely important event occurred which strongly affected the course of both religion and sacred music. Martin Luther (1483-1546), a monk in the Catholic Church, nailed his 95 theses, or attacks against the church, on the cathedral door in Wittenburg, Germany. Thus started the Protestant Reformation. In a few years the Lutheran Church would come into being. Luther, who fully understood the value of music in a worship service, determined to preserve some musical traditions of the past as well as introduce new elements. This combination resulted in the Lutheran *chorale*. Luther either composed his own tunes or borrowed them from Latin hymns, popular, or folk songs. Originally the sturdy, simple tunes were sung in unison. Later they came to be performed in four parts with the melody in the soprano. The most important aspect about the chorale was that it was sung by the congregation in their own language (vernacular) rather than in Latin. Luther felt that music would be a more powerful contribution to worship if the people themselves could participate as much as possible. One of Luther's thirty-seven chorales, "Ein Feste Burg" (A Mighty Fortress), became as it were the *Marseillaise* of the Protestant Reformation.

Several men followed Luther to carry on the trend of chorale composition in Germany. Many of these men were pastors of small Lutheran churches, and their hymns were composed for local rather than universal use. Philipp Nicolai (1556-1608), a pastor, is remembered for two magnificent chorales, "Sleeper's Wake" and "O Morning Star." Martin Rinkart (1586-1649), a great pastor during the Thirty Years' War, wrote the famous "Now Thank We All Our God" in the midst of the struggle. Paul Gerhardt (1607-1676), a minister who was banished to a small country parish after incurring royal disfavor, wrote over one hundred poems for hymns. Joachim Neander (1650-1680), who belonged to the German Reformed Church, greatly enriched Protestant hymnody, his most outstanding contribution being "Praise to the Lord the Almighty." In time Johann Sebastian Bach (1685-1750) would use German chorale melodies extensively in his large choral works and organ compositions. He reharmonized them in the eighteenth century harmonic idiom.

The Moravian movement coincided in time with the Lutheran Reformation. The early leader of the group was Jan Hus (1371-1415), a reformer, who was burned at the stake. His followers formed many small societies which gradually merged into a Brotherhood Unitas Fratum. This brotherhood was characterized by its vitality in singing. In the sixteenth century they published the first hymnbook on the continent, *Mit Freuden Zart*. In 1722, because of severe persecution, they fled to Saxony and built a town called Herrnhut. Count Zinzendorf (1700-1760), their leader at Herrnhut, wrote thousands of hymns for them. From the eighteenth century on, this religious community was known as the Moravians.

John Calvin (1509-1564), who led the reform movement in Switzerland during the Reformation, did not agree with Luther on the use of music in the service. Although both wanted the congregation to participate, the two men drew upon different sources for their worship music. Whereas Luther used Latin hymns and popular tunes with texts from various poets, Calvin thought that only psalms from the Bible and a few New Testament canticles were worthy for use in church. So, Calvin and his followers began to make metrical versions of psalms. Clément Marot and Theodore Beza were two of his versifiers, and Louis Bourgeois (*c.* 1510-*c.* 1561) composed tunes to fit the texts. Their work culminated in the *Genevan Psalter* published in 1562, the most significant compilation of psalms and tunes to be published in its time. It was soon translated into many languages, and was used as a model for metrical psalters published in England, Scotland, and America.

Calvanism was brought back to England by people who had fled to Geneva during the reign of Bloody Mary, who had restored the Catholic faith and burned martyrs. A renowned English psalter was compiled by Thomas Sternhold and John Hopkins in 1567. The *Sternhold and Hopkins Psalter* (the Old Version) adhered strictly to the Hebrew text, and was the accepted Psalm Book for over two hundred years, although the rhymes were sometimes ludicrous. This book was transplanted to America by the Puritans. Then, in 1696, Tate and Brady published *The New Version* of the psalms, but it did not entirely succeed in ousting the *Old Version*, although the rhymes were of better quality.

The metrical psalms were performed unaccompanied by a method called "lining out." A precentor would sing one line and the congregation would answer. The hymns were sung in this manner because most people could not read music. The practice had its drawbacks, however, because the precentor, who had to find his starting pitch unaided, would sometimes start too high or too low. Sometimes he forgot the tune to which a psalm was set and sang a different one. Congregations were encouraged to ornament the tunes, but this soon got out of hand and the original tune was frequently unrecognizable. Gradually, in the eighteenth and nineteenth centuries, the practice of metrical psalm singing declined.

The English hymn evolved as a result of efforts to improve the literary quality of the *Tate and Brady Psalter*. Poets began to paraphrase portions of Scriptures other than the psalms, and then gradually to write completely original texts. Although the Anglican George Herbert (1593-1633) and Thomas Ken (1637-1711) wrote some great hymns, it was Isaac Watts (1674-1748) who did more than anyone to establish hymn singing in English worship services. As a young man Watts reacted strongly against the metrical psalm singing in church. When challenged by his father to write something better, he began his career of hymn writing and produced more than six hundred hymns. Watts felt that the hymns should express the gospel of the New Testament, whether the songs were paraphrases of psalms or freely composed. Further, he believed that hymns should be expressive of the feelings of the worshiper, and not merely recall the experiences of biblical writers. Watts wrote freely, without being bound to literal translations of the Scriptures. He published *Hymns and Spiritual Songs* in 1707 and *The Psalms of David Imitated in the Language of the New Testament and Applied to Christians State and Worship* in 1719. The latter title embodies much of Watts' philosophy regarding hymnody.

Other notable hymnists of Watts' era were Philip Doddridge (1702-1751), a Puritan scholar and poet; Anne Steele (1716-1778), the first woman writer of English hymns; John Fawcett (1740-1817), a famous self-educated Baptist preacher; John Rippon (1751-1836), editor of *Selection of Hymns from the Best Authors, Intended to be a Supplement to Watts' Psalms and Hymns.*

The two outstanding figures of the eighteenth century Evangelical revival in England were John and Charles Wesley, the founders of Methodism. John Wesley (1703-1791) sailed to America in 1735 to visit the Savannah, Georgia, colony. On board the ship he heard a group of Moravians singing, and was so impressed that he learned German in order to converse with them and to make translations from their hymnal. While in Georgia he compiled the first Wesleyan hymnal. When he returned to England, he devoted his time to preaching, organizing his Methodist followers, and editing his brother's hymns.

Charles Wesley (1707-1788) was with John on the ship to Georgia. He spent some time as Governor Oglethorpe's secretary, then returned to England to resume his ministry there through sermon and song. His over six thousand hymns are of high literary quality, and the wide variety of meters he employed was unparalleled at the time. Together the Wesley brothers probably enriched English hymnody to a greater extent than any other men.

Perhaps the most important hymnbook issued as a product of the Evangelical revival was the *Olney Hymns*, compiled by William Cowper (1731-1800) and John Newton (1725-1807). Newton and Cowper preached, taught, and wrote together, and it is quite likely that this relationship aided the frail and neurotic Cowper in keeping his sanity.

Among British hymn writers of importance who were contemporaries of the Wesleys were: William Williams (1717-1791), an Evangelical convert; Edward Perronet (1726-1792), who disagreed with the Methodists and allied himself with the Calvinistic philosophy; Augustus Toplady (1740-1778), who also disagreed with John Wesley, as evident throughout his sermons and written articles.

The nineteenth century, the Romantic Age, brought a new emphasis on lyric expression, emotion, and imagination with regard to religious poetry. The outstanding hymnist of the period was Bishop Reginald Heber (1783-1826) who compiled a hymnbook in which the hymns were arranged according to the church year outlined in the Anglican Prayer Book. Other significant writers were Reverend John Keble (1792-1866) who published a book of nature poems, *Christian Year;* Robert Grant (1779-1838), the Governor of Bombay; Charlotte Elliott (1789-1871), an invalid whose hymns were characterized by a tender sweetness; John Bowring (1792-1872), who was knighted for social and political achievements; Henry Francis Lyte (1793-1847), an Anglican parson of a tiny fishing village.

The third decade of the nineteenth century saw the beginning of the Oxford Movement in which several Anglican church leaders such as John Keble and John Henry Newman (1801-1890) tried to revive the dignity and attractiveness of the Church of England by purifying its worship services. The Oxford Movement affected the clergy as well as the music. It was felt that liturgical hymns which expressed the voice of the church and were related to its holidays and hours of worship, should be used rather than the evangelical hymns which voiced the experience of an individual. As a result of the Oxford Movement, there was a revival of interest in pre-Reformation Latin and Greek hymns. A treasury of medieval hymns—translated by Edward Caswall (1814-1878), Frances E. Cox (1812-1897), John Ellerton (1801-1873), Catherine Winkworth (1829-1878), and John Mason Neale (1818-1876)—was among the most significant contributions to this movement. The famous 1861 collection, *Hymns Ancient and Modern,* by William Henry Monk (1823-1889) also emerged as a result of the Oxford Revival. The book, which did not include any hymns of evangelical origin, was used by the majority of churches. This managed to unify the church's hymnody somewhat, and to allow the book to become a national institution in England.

Since the early American settlers came to the shores of the New World at the time the Calvinistic practice of metrical psalm singing was prevalent in England, they brought psalters with them. The Puritans brought the *Sternhold and Hopkins Psalter* while the Pilgrims, who had fled to Holland before leaving for America, brought the *Ainsworth Psalter,* which had been especially prepared for them in Amsterdam by Henry Ainsworth. However, in 1640 in Cambridge, Massachusetts three ministers published a retranslation of the psalms known as the *Bay Psalm Book.* It was the first publication of any kind by an English speaking colony in the New World.

Psalm singing in colonial churches was performed in the same manner as in English churches of the period, which means that the unsatisfactory method of "lining out" was retained. In time, tunes became so distorted that some ministers urged that people learn to read notes in order that congregational singing might be improved.

Two things aided the people's musical education. Instruction books were written which taught various methods for note reading. One method, which was particularly popular in the South and West in the nineteenth century, introduced shaped note heads. A different shaped note represented the four syllables (fa, sol, la, mi) then used. Later, shapes for the remaining three syllables (do, re, ti) were added. Of the tune books which utilized the four-shaped notation, William Walker's *Southern Harmony* and Benjamin White's *Sacred Harp* were the most widely used.

A second development in the effort to upgrade the quality of congregational singing was the establishment of singing schools. These schools provided both an educational and recreational outlet for adults and children in the evening. Usually led by a traveling singing master, the groups learned to read from shaped note hymnals, and gave concerts at the termination of their instruction. Members of the singing schools then went on to become members of their various church choirs.

One of the outstanding leaders of a Massachusetts singing school was William Billings (1746-1800). A tanner by trade and a self-taught musician, Billings is known today as the first native American composer.

Elsewhere in colonial America, the Moravians, who eventually made their home in

Bethlehem, Pennsylvania, had a more highly developed musical life than any other group of settlers. However, because they spoke a different language, and were of a different culture from the majority of the colonists, their influence on the American Christian hymn was slight.

The transition from psalmody to hymnody took place in the eighteenth century, and the nineteenth century brought a flood of hymn writers to the American scene. Lowell Mason (1792-1872), the founder of public school music, did much to improve church music in Boston by beginning children's music classes in church and by publishing song books. Thomas Hastings (1787-1872), another man who wanted to raise the standard of church music, wrote six hundred hymns toward that end.

Some of the finest nineteenth century hymns flowed from the pens of Unitarian preachers and poets. Oliver Wendell Holmes (1809-1894), John Greenleaf Whittier (1807-1892), and James Russell Lowell (1819-1891) whose literary merits are well-known, wrote humanitarian hymns for congregational use.

A special feature of American religious life in the 1800's was the camp meeting, which spread through most of the East. One of the outstanding characteristics of the meetings was the enthusiastic singing of songs often spontaneously composed. The songs, generally in ballad style with a repeated refrain or chorus, were folk-like and easy to learn.

From the camp-meeting songs and the songs of the singing schools came the gospel song. In contrast to the solemn, often intricate melodies of psalmody, gospel hymns had simple, catchy melodies, and the texts expressed Christian experience in emotional, everyday language. The songs, quickly learned and easily remembered, appealed to millions. There were over a thousand gospel song books issued in the nineteenth century, and the names of Dwight L. Moody and Ira D. Sankey (1840-1908) are forever linked with this American sacred music form.

The first gospel hymnbook was *Hallowed Songs* published by Phillip Phillips (1834-1895). Ira Sankey used this in England where he and Dwight Moody had their first great success. On returning to America they united Sankey's *Sacred Songs and Solos* with a collection of songs by Philip Paul Bliss (1838-1876), a prominent evangelist-singer. This merger resulted in *Hymns and Sacred Songs*.

The most prolific author of gospel hymns was Fanny Crosby (1820-1915), who wrote from the early 1850's until her death at the age of ninety-five.

OTHER SACRED FORMS

In the Middle ages, from about the seventh century on, church music was dominated by Gregorian Chant, so called because the melodies were collected and codified during the reign of Pope Gregory. Gregorian Chant, derived from Greek and Hebrew music, is sometimes called plainsong because it consists of a single unaccompanied vocal line of melody. This melody flows freely with no regular accent, and the duration or length of the tones being closely allied with the text, are almost equally free. To modern listeners these chants lack melodic, dynamic, and rhythmic excitement. Plainsong is not composed within our present system of major and minor tonality, but is based on one of eight church modes, the intervals of which correspond to scales played on the white keys of the piano only.

Gregorian chant is still used in the celebration of the Catholic Mass today, although now the texts are not only in Latin, but in the vernacular as well. The Mass, the principal form of the Catholic worship service, consists of prayers, scripture lessons, hymns, and responses. Those elements that remain unaltered in the Mass are called the Ordinary. Composers throughout history have set the texts of the Ordinary to music: *Kyrie, Gloria, Credo, Sanctus, Agnus Dei.* (The parts of the Mass that change according to the holiday or season are called the Proper.)

In the medieval period monophonic (a single line of melody such as found in Gregorian chant) Masses were composed. By the fifteenth century, composers such as the Englishman John Dunstable (1370?-1453) and Guillaume Dufay, the Flemish composer (c. 1398-1474), were writing polyphonic (more than one line of melody) settings. Later exponents of polyphony included Flemish Composers Josquin Des Prés (c. 1445-1521) and Jakob Obrecht (c.1430-1505). However, the polyphonic Mass reached its peak of perfection in the Renaissance period with the Italian master Giovanni Pierluigi da Palestrina (c. 1524-1594). Palestrina's Masses were selected as models for Catholic church music by the participants in the Council of Trent.

After the seventeenth century, Masses had instrumental accompaniment. Composers such as Mozart (1756-1791), Haydn (1732-1809), Beethoven (1772-1827), Schubert (1797-1828), and Cherubini (1760-1842) scored some of their Masses for full orchestra.

There are two special types of Masses that differ in format from the regular Mass. The Requiem Mass, or Mass for the dead, substitutes more solemn texts for the joyful portions of the Mass. Berlioz (1803-1869), Verdi (1813-1901), Brahms (1833-1897), Mozart, and Gabriel Fauré (1845-1924) have contributed enduring compositions to this field. Another special type is the *Missa Brevis*. To the Lutherans the term meant that only the *Kyrie* and the *Gloria* were used. However, in southern Germany and Austria the *Missa Brevis* contained all of the Ordinary, but without elaborate instrumentation or ornamentation, and repetitions were avoided where possible.

It is difficult to find a single adequate definition for the *motet* since it was quite different in each period of its development. Generally speaking, the motet is a part song for unaccompanied voices that is sung (usually in Latin) during a worship service. (The term motet comes from the French "mot" meaning "word.")

Josquin Des Prés, an outstanding motet composer of the Renaissance, was known for a process called "points of imitation." In this type of composition each phrase of text is given a distinctive musical idea which is then imitated in every voice when the same text occurs. Although independent melodies which overlap and produce a polyphonic texture are the norm, sometimes chordal or homophonic sections are inserted between the imitative sections. Other great motet composers of the period were the Spaniard Tomás Luis de Victoria (1548-1611), the Englishman William Byrd (1543-1623), and the Flemish composer, Orlando di Lasso (1532-1594).

Although the motet form declined in popularity after the Renaissance, some prominent composers continued to write in this vein; J. S. Bach, Mozart, Brahms, Vaughan Williams (1872-1958), Poulenc (1899-1963), and Randall Thompson (1899-   ) have all made use of the form.

Cantata comes from the Italian "cantare" meaning "to sing." It is an instrumentally accompanied vocal composition in several movements which is usually sacred, and meant to be performed as part of a worship service. Although it developed in Italy, this form is best known today through the work of J. S. Bach, who left more than three hundred cantatas. He wrote five sets of them, each set containing a cantata for every Sunday of the liturgical year. In addition to this monumental output, Bach composed several secular cantatas for special occasions. The characteristic movements of the Bach cantatas were either full choruses, solos, or duets. The solo music, influenced by the then popular style of opera, was in the form of recitatives or arias. Many of Bach's sacred cantatas were based on traditional Lutheran chorales. The cantata, which all but disappeared after Bach, has been gaining favor again with composers in the twentieth century.

The Oratorio, another important choral form of the Baroque period, is quite similar to the cantata. An oratorio is longer, however, and although the text is usually sacred, it is non-liturgical, and therefore not meant to be performed in a worship service. The history of the form goes back to sixteenth-century Italy during the time of St. Philip Neri (1515-1595), who gave sacred dramas with music in his prayer chapel or oratory. The outstanding composer of this form as we know it today was George Frederick Handel (1685-1759) who, when his operas were failing to draw the English public, began to compose religious musical dramas which people could attend during the Lenten season. An oratorio in the Handelian tradition is very dramatic, and all but two of his epics relate stories from the Old Testament. His greatest masterpiece, *Messiah*, a beautiful lyric work contemplating the life of Christ, is an exception rather than the rule with Handel.

A special type of oratorio, based on the Easter story from one of the four gospels, is called a Passion. The German composer Heinrich Schütz (1585-1672) is noted for his compositions of this type. Bach's compositions based on the passions according to St. Matthew and St. John are among music's priceless treasures.

The oratorio continued in England and on the continent after Handel in the gifted hands of Haydn (1732-1809), Mendelssohn (1809-1847), Parry (1848-1918), Elgar (1857-1934), and Honneger (1892-1955).

The anthem developed in England as a substitute for the Latin motet. At first English words merely substituted for the Latin, but at other times, entirely new compositions were created. By the seventeenth century there were two types of anthems: the full anthem in which the choir sang throughout; and the verse anthem in which solo voices appeared alternately with the chorus. Significant anthem composers of the past were Orlando Gibbons (1583-1625), William Byrd (1543-1623), Thomas Morley (1557-1603), John Blow (1648-1708), Henry Purcell (*c.* 1659-1695), and Samuel Wesley (1810-1876). Many contemporary composers are represented in worship services by very distinguished anthems.

It seems that in every age in every place men have been obedient to the psalmist's exhortation to "sing unto the Lord."

Contents

THE
INTERNATIONAL BOOK
OF
SACRED SONG

American

America The Beautiful

KATHERINE LEE BATES (1859–1929)

SAMUEL A. WARD (1847–1903)

1. O beau-ti-ful for spa-cious skies, For am-ber waves of grain,
2. O beau-ti-ful for pil-grim feet, Whose stern im-pas-sioned stress,

For pur-ple moun-tain maj-es-ties A-bove the fruit-ed plain!
A thor-ough-fare for free-dom beat A-cross the wil-der-ness!

A-mer-i-ca! A-mer-i-ca! God shed His grace on thee,___
A-mer-i-ca! A-mer-i-ca! God mend thine ev-ery flaw,___

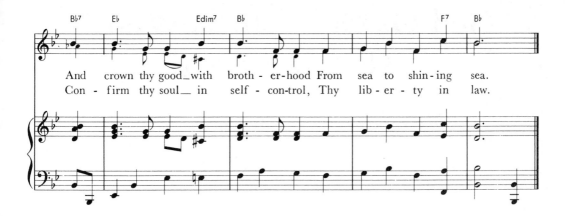

And crown thy good_with broth - er-hood From sea to shin - ing sea.
Con - firm thy soul_ in self - con-trol, Thy lib - er - ty in law.

3. O beautiful for heroes proved
   In liberating strife,
   Who more than self their country loved,
   And mercy more than life!
   America! America!
   May God thy gold refine,
   Till all success be nobleness,
   And every gain divine.

4. O beautiful for patriot dream,
   That sees, beyond the years,
   Thine alabaster cities gleam,
   Undimmed by human tears!
   America! America!
   God shed His grace on thee,
   And crown thy good with brotherhood,
   From sea to shining sea.

God Of Our Fathers Whose Almighty Hand

DANIEL C. ROBERTS (1841–1907)

GEORGE W. WARREN (1828–1902)

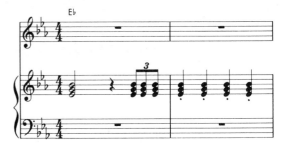

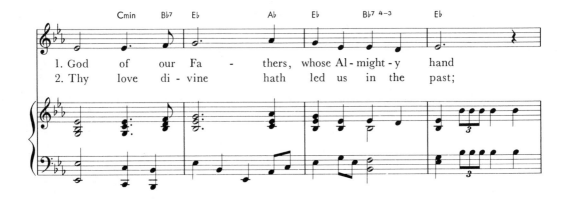

1. God of our Fa - thers, whose Al - might - y hand
2. Thy love di - vine hath led us in the past;

Leads forth in beau - ty all the star - ry band
In this free land by Thee our lot is cast;

Of   shin - ing worlds   in   splen-dor through the   skies,
Be   Thou our   rul - er,   guard-ian, guide, and   stay,

Our   grate - ful songs   be - fore Thy throne a - rise.
Thy   word our law,   Thy   paths our   cho - sen way.

3. From war's alarms, from deadly pestilence,
    Be Thy strong arm our ever sure defense;
    Thy true religion in our hearts increase,
    Thy bounteous goodness nourish us in peace.

4. Refresh Thy people on their toilsome way;
    Lead us from night to never ending day;
    Fill all our lives with love and grace divine,
    And glory, laud, and praise be ever Thine.

Battle Hymn Of The Republic

JULIA WARD HOWE (1819–1910)   AMERICAN FOLK SONG

1. Mine___ eyes have seen the glo - ry of the com - ing of the Lord;
2. I have seen Him in the watch - fires of a hun - dred cir - cling camps;

He is tramp-ling out the vin - tage where the grapes of wrath are stored;
They have build - ed Him an al - tar in the eve - ning dews and damps;

He hath loosed the fate - ful light - ning of His ter - ri - ble swift sword;
I can read His right-eous sen - tence by the dim and flar - ing lamps;

His truth is march-ing on.
His day is march-ing on.

Glo - ry! glo - ry, hal - le - lu - jah!

Glo - ry! glo - ry, hal - le - lu - jah!

Glo - ry! glo - ry, hal - le -

lu - jah! Our God is march - ing on.

3. He has sounded forth the trumpet that shall never sound retreat;
   He is sifting out the hearts of men before His judgment seat;
   O be swift, my soul, to answer Him! be jubilant, my feet!
   Our God is marching on.   (*Refrain*)

4. In the beauty of the lilies, Christ was born across the sea,
   With a glory in His bosom that transfigures you and me;
   As He died to make men holy, let us die to make men free,
   While God is marching on.   (*Refrain*)

This Is My Father's World

MALTBIE D. BABCOCK (1858–1901)

TRAD. ENGLISH MELODY
ARR. BY FRANKLIN L. SHEPPARD, 1915

Of__ rocks and trees, of____ skies and seas; His hand__ the__ won-ders__ wrought.
In the rust-ling grass I____ hear Him pass, He speaks_ to__ me ev-ery-where.
The__ Lord is King: Let the heav-ens ring! God reigns:_ let the earth be__ glad!

Ancient Of Days

WILLIAM C. DOANE (1832–1913)

J. ALBERT JEFFERY (1851–1928)

1. An - cient of Days, who sit - test throned in glo - ry,
2. O Ho - ly Fa - ther, who hast led Thy chil - dren
3. O Tri - une God, with heart and voice a - dor - ing,

To Thee all knees are bent, all voic - es pray; Thy love has blessed the
In all the a - ges with the fire and cloud. Through seas dry - shod, through
Praise we the good - ness that doth crown our days; Pray we that Thou wilt

Wide world's won-drous sto - ry With light and life since E - den's dawn - ing day.
Wea - ry wastes be - wil - dering: To Thee in rev - erent love our hearts are bowed.
Hear us, still im - plor - ing Thy love and fa - vor kept to us al - ways.

Dear Lord And Father Of Mankind

JOHN G. WHITTIER (1807–1892)   FREDERICK C. MAKER (1844–1927)

1. Dear Lord and Fa - ther of man - kind, For - give our fool - ish
2. Drop Thy still dews of qui - et - ness, till all our striv - ings
3. Breathe through the heats of our de - sire Thy cool - ness and Thy

ways; Re - clothe us in our right - ful minds, In
cease; Take from our souls the strain and stress, And
balm; Let sense be dumb, let flesh re - tire; Speak

pur - er lives Thy ser - vice find, In deep - er rev - 'rence, praise.
let our or - dered lives con - fess The beau - ty of Thy peace.
through the earth - quake, wind and fire, O still, small voice of calm!

Rock Of Ages, Cleft For Me

AUGUSTUS M. TOPLADY (1740–1778)　　　　　　　　　　　　THOMAS HASTINGS (1784–1872)

1. Rock of A - ges, cleft for me, Let me hide my - self in Thee;
2. Could my tears for - ev - er flow, Could my zeal no lan - gour know;
3. While I draw this fleet-ing breath, When my eyes shall close in death;

Let the wa - ter and the blood, from Thy wound - ed side which flowed,
These for sin could not a - tone, Thou must save, and Thou a - lone;
When I rise to worlds un - known, And be - hold Thee on Thy throne;

Be of sin the dou - ble cure, Save from wrath and make me pure.
In my hand no price I bring; Sim - ply to Thy cross I cling.
Rock of A - ges cleft for me, Let me hide my - self in Thee.

O My Father

ELIZA R. SNOW

JAMES MC GRANAHAN

1. O__ my Fa - ther, Thou__that dwell - est in__ the high_____ and glo - rious
2. For__ a wise and glo - rious pur - pose Thou__hast placed_____ me here__on

place,__ When__shall I re - gain__Thy pres - ence and__a - gain_____ be hold__ thy
earth,__ And__with-held the rec - ol - lec - tion of__my for - mer friends and

In Thy ho - ly hab - i - ta - tion, Did__ my
Yet oft - times_____ a se - cret some - thing, Whis - pered,

face?____ In Thy ho - ly hab - i - ta - tion,
birth,____ Yet oft-times a se - cret some - thing,

3. I had learned to call Thee Father, Through Thy Spirit from on high;
   But unto the key of knowledge Was restored, I knew not why.
   In the heavens are parents single? No, the thought makes reasons stare!
   Truth is reason, truth eternal Tells me I've a mother there.

4. When I leave this frail existence, When I lay this mortal by
   Father, Mother, may I meet you, In your royal courts on high?
   Then, at length, when I've completed All you sent me forth to do,
   With your mutual approbation Let me come and dwell with you.

Nearer, My God, To Thee

SARAH F. ADAMS (1805–1848)

LOWELL MASON (1792–1872)

Near - er, my God to Thee, Near - er to Thee.
Near - er, my God to Thee, Near - er to Thee.
Near - er, my God to Thee, Near - er to Thee.

Rejoice, Ye Pure In Heart

EDWARD H. PLUMPTRE (1821–1891)   ARTHUR H. MESSITER (1831–1916)

1. Re - joice, ye pure in heart, Re - joice, give thanks and sing;
2. Bright youth and snow-crowned age, Strong men, and maid - ens fair,
3. Still lift your stan - dard high, Still march in firm ar - ray,

Your glo - rious banner wave on high, The cross of Christ your King.
Raise high your free, ex - ult - ing song, God's won-drous praise de - clare.
As war - riors thro' the dark - ness toil, Till dawns the gold - en day.

REFRAIN

Re - joice, (re - joice) Re - joice, (re - joice) Re - joice, Give thanks and sing.

Gently Raise The Sacred Strain

W. W. PHELPS

THOMAS C. GRIGGS

1. Gent - ly raise the sa - cred strain, For the
2. Ho - ly day de - void of strife; Let us

Sab - bath's come a - gain That man may rest, That man may
Seek e - ter - nal life, That great re - ward, That great re -

rest, And re - turn his thanks to God For His Bless - ings
ward, And par - take the sac - ra - ment In re - mem - brance

to the blest, For___ His Bless - ings to the blest.
of our Lord, In___ re - mem - brance of our Lord.

3. Sweetly swells the solemn sound,
   While we bring our gifts around
   Of broken hearts, of broken hearts,
   As a willing sacrifice,
   Showing what His grace imparts,
   Showing what His grace imparts.

4. Happy type of things to come,
   When the Saints are gathered home
   To praise the Lord, to praise the Lord,
   In eternity of bliss,
   All as one with sweet accord,
   All as one with sweet accord.

As The Dew From Heaven Distilling

PARLEY P. PRATT

JOSEPH J. DAYNES

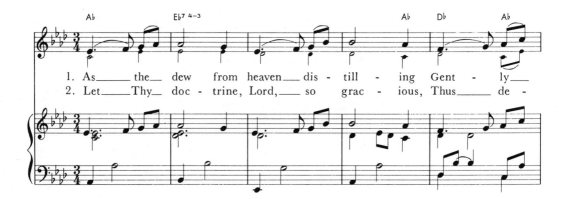

1. As____ the__ dew from heaven__ dis - till - ing Gent - ly__
2. Let____Thy__ doc - trine, Lord,___ so grac - ious, Thus____ de -

on the grass____ de - scends____ And re - vives____ it,
scend - ing from____ a - bove,____ Blest by__ Thee,____ prove

thus ful - fill - ing What___ thy___ prov - i - dence in - tends.
ef - fi - ca - cious To___ ful - fill___ Thy___ work of___ love.

3. Lord, behold this congregation;
   Precious promises fulfill;
   From Thy holy habitation
   Let the dews of life distill.

4. Let our cry come up before Thee;
   Thy sweet Spirit shed around,
   So the people shall adore Thee
   And confess the joyful sound.

Sweet Hour Of Prayer

WILLIAM W. WALFORD

WILLIAM B. BRADBURY (1816–1868)

1. Sweet hour of prayer, sweet hour of prayer! That calls me from a world of care,
2. Sweet hour of prayer, sweet hour of prayer! The joys I feel, the bliss I share,
3. Sweet hour of prayer, sweet hour of prayer! The wings shall my petition bear,

And bids me at my Father's throne Make all my wants and wishes known;
Of those whose anxious spirits burn With strong desires for Thy return!
To Him whose truth and faithfulness Engage the waiting soul to bless;

In seasons of distress and grief, My soul has often found relief;
With such I hasten to the place, Where God my Saviour shows His face,
And since He bids me seek His face, Believe His word and trust His grace,

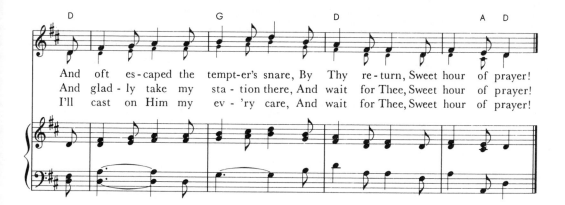

And oft es-caped the tempt-er's snare, By Thy re-turn, Sweet hour of prayer!
And glad-ly take my sta-tion there, And wait for Thee, Sweet hour of prayer!
I'll cast on Him my ev-'ry care, And wait for Thee, Sweet hour of prayer!

Amazing Grace

JOHN NEWTON (1725–1807)

EARLY AMERICAN MELODY

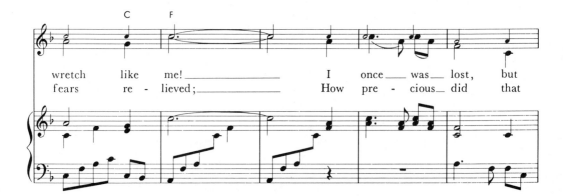

1. A - maz - ing grace! How sweet the sound That saved a
2. 'Twas grace that taught my heart to fear. And grace my

wretch like me! I once was lost, but
fears re - lieved; How pre - cious did that

now___ am___ found, Was blind, but___ now I see.___
grace___ ap - pear The hour I ___ first be - lieved!___

3. Through many dangers, toils, and snares,
   I have already come;
   'Tis grace hath brought me safe thus far,
   And grace will lead me home.

4. The Lord hath promised good to me,
   His word my hope secures;
   He will my shield and portion be
   As long as life endures.

Blessed Assurance

FANNY J. CROSBY (1820–1915)   MRS. JOSEPH F. KNAPP (1839–1898)

1. Bless-ed as - sur - ance, Je - sus is mine! O what a fore-taste of glo-ry di - vine! Heir of sal - va - tion, pur-chase of God, Born of His Spir - it, saved by His word.

2. Per - fect sub - mis - sion, Per - fect de - light, Vi - sions of rap - ture now burst on my sight; An-gels de - scend - ing, bring from a - bove, Ech - oes of mer - cy, whis-pers of love.

3. Per - fect sub - mis - sion, All is at rest, I in my Sav - iour am hap-py and blest, Watch-ing and wait - ing, look-ing a - bove, Filled with His mer - cy, lost in His love.

REFRAIN

This is my sto - ry, this is my song, ____ Prais - ing my

Sav - iour all the day long; ____ This is my sto - ry, this is my

song, ____ Prais - ing my Sav - iour all the day long. ____

Love Divine, All Loves Excelling

CHARLES WESLEY (1707–1788)

JOHN ZUNDEL (1815–1882)

1. Love di - vine, all loves ex - cell - ing, Joy of heaven to earth come down;
2. Breathe, O breathe Thy lov - ing spir - it In - to ev - ery trou - bled breast!

Fix in us Thy hum - ble dwell - ing, All Thy faith - ful mer - cies crown!
Let us all in Thee in - her - it Let us find the prom - ised rest;

Je - sus, Thou art all com - pas - sion, Pure un - bound - ed love Thou art,
Take a - way our bent to sin - ning; Al - pha and O - me - ga be;

Vis - it us with Thy sal - va - tion, En - ter ev - 'ry trem-bling heart.
End of faith, as its be - gin - ning, Set our hearts at lib - er - ty.

3. Come, Almighty to deliver, Let us all Thy grace receive;
   Suddenly return, and never, Never more Thy temples leave.
   Thee we would be always blessing, Serve Thee as Thy hosts above,
   Pray, and praise Thee without ceasing, Glory in Thy perfect love.

4. Finish, then, Thy new creation; Pure and spotless let us be;
   Let us see Thy great salvation Perfectly restored in Thee:
   Changed from glory into glory, Till in heaven we take our place,
   Till we cast our crowns before Thee, Lost in wonder, love and praise.

My Faith Looks Up To Thee

RAY PALMER (1808–1887)

LOWELL MASON (1792–1872)

1. My faith looks up to Thee, Thou Lamb of Cal - va - ry,
2. May Thy rich grace im-part, Strength to my faint - ing heart,

Sav - iour di - vine! Now hear me while I pray, Take all my
My zeal in - spire! As Thou hast died for me, O may my

guilt a - way, O let me from this day Be whol - ly Thine.
love to Thee, Pure, warm and change-less be, A liv - ing fire!

3. While life's dark maze I tread, And griefs around me spread,
   Be Thou my guide;
   Bid darkness turn to day, Wipe sorrow's tears away.
   Nor let me ever stray, From Thee aside.

4. When ends life's transient dream, When death's cold sullen, stream
   Shall o'er me roll;
   Blest Saviour, then, in love, Fear and distrust remove;
   O bear me safe above, A ransomed soul!

I Love To Tell The Story

KATHERINE HANKEY (1834–1911)

WILLIAM G. FISCHER (1835–1912)

1. I love to tell the sto - ry, Of un - seen things_ a - bove,
2. I love to tell the sto - ry; 'Tis pleas - ant to__ re - peat,
3. I love to tell the sto - ry, For those who know_ it best,

Of Je - sus and His glo - ry. Of__ Je - sus and__ His love,
What seems, each time I tell it, More__ won - der - ful - ly sweet.
Seem hun - ger-ing and thirst-ing, To__ hear it like__ the rest.

I love to tell the sto - ry Be - cause I know 'tis__ true;
I love to tell the sto - ry For some have nev - er__ heard,
And when, in scenes of glo - ry, I sing the new, new__ song,

It sat - is - fies my long - ings As noth - ing else can do.
The mes - sage of sal - va - tion From God's own ho - ly word.
'Twill be the old, old sto - ry That I have loved so long.

REFRAIN

I love to tell the sto - ry, 'Twill be my theme in glo - ry,

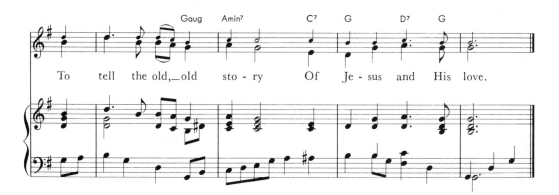

To tell the old,—old sto - ry Of Je - sus and His love.

Into The Woods My Master Went

SIDNEY LANIER (1841–1881)

PETER L. LUTKIN (1858–1931)

1. In - to the woods__ my Mas - ter went,___ Clean for-spent, for - spent;___
2. Out of the woods__ my Mas - ter went, And He was well con - tent;___

In - to the woods__ my Mas - ter came, For - spent with love__ and shame.___ But the
Out of the woods__ my Mas - ter came, Con - tent with death__ and shame.___ When__

Ol - ives they were not blind to Him, The lit - tle gray leaves__ were kind to Him, The
death and shame__ would woo Him last, From un - der the trees__ they drew Him last, 'Twas

thorn tree had___ a mind to Him, When in - to the woods He came.
on   a   tree___ they slew Him last, When out of the woods He came.

What A Friend We Have In Jesus

JOSEPH SCRIVEN (1820–1886)

CHARLES C. CONVERSE (1832–1918)

1. What a friend we have in Je - sus, All our sins and griefs to bear!
2. Have we tri - als and temp - ta - tions? Is there trou - ble an - y - where?
3. Are we weak and heav - y la - den, Cum - bered with a load of care?

What a priv - i - lege to car - ry Ev - 'ry thing to God in prayer!
We should nev - er be dis - cour - aged: Take it to the Lord in prayer.
Pre - cious Sav - iour, still our ref - uge; Take it to the Lord in prayer.

O what peace we of - ten for - feit, O what need - less pain we bear,
Can we find a friend so faith - ful, Who will all our trou - bles share?
Do thy friends de - spise, for - sake thee? Take it to the Lord in prayer!

All be-cause we do not car - ry Ev - 'ry-thing to God in prayer!
Je - sus knows our ev-'ry weak - ness, Take it to the Lord in prayer!
In His arms He'll take and shield thee, Thou wilt find a sol - ace there.

All Hail The Power Of Jesus' Name

EDWARD PERRONET (1726–1792)
ALT. JOHN RIPPON (1751–1836)

OLIVER HOLDEN (1765–1844)

1. All hail the power of Je - sus' Name! Let an - gels pros - trate fall;
2. Ye cho - sen seed of Is - rael's race, Ye ran - somed from the fall,
3. Let ev - 'ry kin - dred, ev -'ry tribe, On this ter - res - trial ball,

Bring forth the roy - al di - a - dem
Hail Him who saves you by_ His_ grace, And crown Him Lord of_ all;
To Him all maj - es - ty_ as - cribe,

Bring forth the roy - al di - a - dem,
Hail Him who saves you by_ His_ grace, And crown Him Lord_ of all.
To Him all maj - es - ty_ as - cribe,

How Firm A Foundation

"K" IN RIPPON'S SELECTION, 1787

EARLY AMERICAN MELODY

1. How firm a foun-da-tion, ye saints of the Lord, Is laid for your
2. "Fear not, I am with Thee; O be not dis-mayed, for I am thy
3. "The soul that on Je-sus still leans for re-pose, I will not, I

Faith in His ex-cel-lent word! What more can He say than to
God and will still give thee aid; I'll strength-en thee, help thee, and
will not de-sert to his foes; That soul, though all hell should en-

you He hath said, to you who for ref-uge to Je-sus have fled?
cause thee to stand, up-held by my right-eous, om-nip-o-tent hand.
deav-or to shake, I'll nev-er, no, nev-er, no nev-er for-sake!"

I Would Be True

HOWARD A. WALTER (1883–1918)

JOSEPH Y. PEEK (1841–1911)

1. I would be true, for there are those who trust me;
2. I would be friend of all the foe, the friend-less;
3. I would be prayer-ful through each bus-y mo-ment;

I would be Pure, For there are those who care;
I would be Giv-ing and for-get the gift;
I would be Con-stant-ly in touch with God;

I would be strong, For There is much to suf-fer;
I would be hum-ble For I know my weak-ness;
I would be tuned to Hear the slight-est whis-per;

I would be brave for there is much to dare.
I would look up, and laugh, and love and lift.
I would have faith, to keep the path Christ trod,

I would be brave, for there is much to dare.
I would look up, and laugh, and love and lift.
I would have faith, to keep the path Christ trod.

Blest Be The Tie That Binds

JOHN FAWCETT (1740–1817)

MELODY: HANS NÄGELI (1768–1836)
ARR. BY LOWELL MASON (1792–1872)

1. Blest be___ the tie___ that binds Our hearts___ in
2. Be - fore___ our Fa - ther's throne We pour___ our

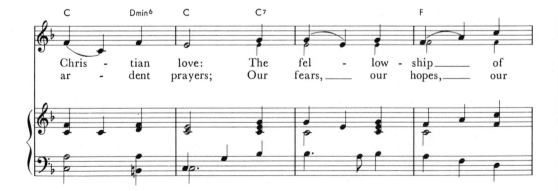

Chris - tian love: The fel - low - ship___ of
ar - dent prayers; Our fears,___ our hopes,___ our

kin - dred minds _____ Is like _____ to that _____ a - bove.
aims _____ are one, _____ Our com - forts and _____ our cares.

3.   We share each other's woes,
        Each other's burdens bear,
        And often for each other flows
        The sympathetic tear.

4.   When we are called to part,
        It gives us inward pain;
        But we shall still be joined in heart,
        And hope to meet again.

O Brother Man

JOHN G. WHITTIER (1807–1892)

JOSEPH W. LERMAN (1865–1935)

1. O broth-er man, fold to thy heart thy broth-er!____ Where pit-y dwells, the peace of God is there;____ To wor-ship right-ly is to love each oth-er,____ Each smile a hymn, each kind-ly deed a prayer.

2. For he whom Je-sus loved hath tru-ly spo-ken;____ The ho-lier wor-ship which He deigns to bless;____ Re-stores the lost, and binds the spir-it bro-ken,____ And feeds the wid-ow and the fa-ther-less.

3. Fol-low with rev-'rent steps the great ex-am-ple____ Of Him whose ho-ly work was do-ing good;____ So shall the wide earth seem our Fa-ther's tem-ple,____ Each lov-ing life a psalm of grat-i-tude.

Rise Up, O Men Of God

WILLIAM PEARSON MERRILL (1867–1954)   AARON WILLIAMS (1731–1776)

1. Rise up, O men of__ God! Have__ done with__ less - er things;
2. Rise up, O men of__ God! His__ king-dom__ tar - ries long;

Give heart and soul and mind and strength To serve the__ King of kings.
Bring in the day of broth - er - hood, And end the__ night of wrong.

3. Rise up, O men of God! The Church for you doth wait,
   Her strength unequal to her task; Rise up and make her great!

4. Lift high the cross of Christ! Tread where His feet have trod;
   As brothers of the Son of man, Rise up, O men of God!

Where Cross The Crowded Ways Of Life

FRANK MASON NORTH (1850–1935)

FROM WILLIAM GARDINER'S
Sacred Melodies, 1815

1. Where cross the crowd - ed ways___ of life, Where sound the
2. In haunts of wretch - ed - ness ___ and need, On shad - owed

cries of race___ and clan, A - bove the noise___ of
thresh - olds dark___ with fears, from paths where hide___ the

self - ish— strife,— We hear Thy voice,— O Son— of man!
lures of— greed,— We catch the vi - sion of— Thy tears.

3. The cup of water given for Thee
   Still holds the freshness of Thy grace;
   Yet long these multitudes to see
   The sweet compassion of Thy face.

4. O Master, from the mountainside,
   Make haste to heal these hearts of pain;
   Among these restless throngs abide,
   O tread the city's streets again.

Come, Come, Ye Saints

WILLIAM CLAYTON

OLD ENGLISH TUNE

1. Come, come, ye saints, no toil nor la-bor fear; But with joy
2. Why should we mourn or think our lot is hard? 'Tis not so;

wend your way. Though hard to you this jour-ney may ap-pear,
all is right. Why should we think to earn a great re-ward,

Grace shall be as your day. 'Tis____ bet-ter far_____ for
If we now shun the fight? Gird____ up your loins,_____ Fresh

48

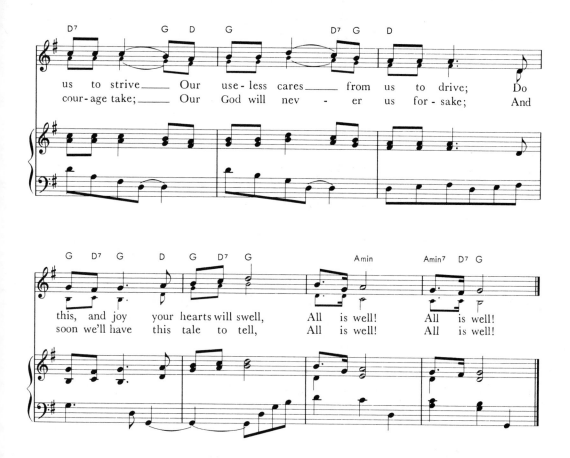

us to strive_____ Our use-less cares_____ from us to drive; Do
cour-age take;_____ Our God will nev - er us for-sake; And

this, and joy your hearts will swell, All is well! All is well!
soon we'll have this tale to tell, All is well! All is well!

3. We'll find the place which God for us prepared,
    Far away in the west,
    Where none shall come to hurt or make afraid;
    There the saints will be blessed.
    We'll make the air with music ring; Shout praises to our God and King;
    Above the rest these words we'll tell: All is well, All is well!

4. And should we die before our journey's through,
    Happy day! All is well!
    We then are free from toil and sorrow, too;
    With the just we shall dwell!
    But if our lives are spared again, To see the saints their rest obtain,
    O how we'll make this chorus swell: All is well, All is well!

Simple Gifts

SHAKER HYMN

'Tis the gift to be sim-ple, 'Tis the gift to be free, 'Tis the gift to come down where we ought to be, And when we find our-selves in the place just___ right, 'Twill___ be in the val-ley of love and de-light, When true sim-pli-ci-ty is gained, to

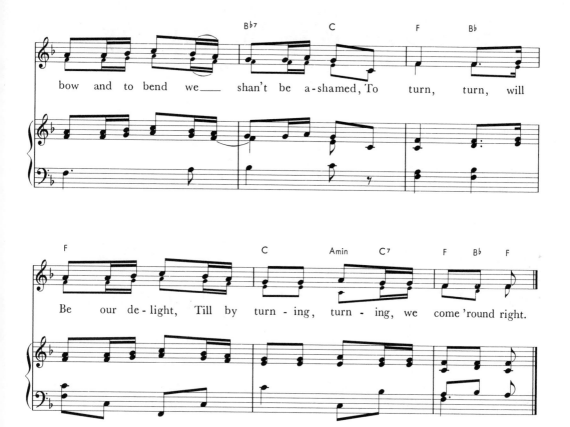

bow and to bend we___ shan't be a-shamed, To turn, turn, will
Be our de-light, Till by turn-ing, turn-ing, we come 'round right.

My Shepherd Will Supply My Need

Based on Psalm 23

AMERICAN FOLK HYMN

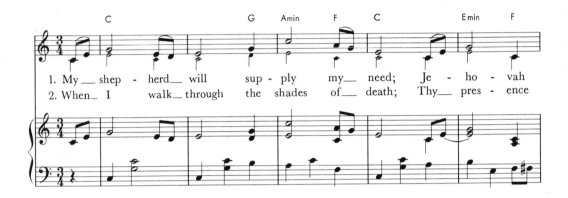

1. My — shep - herd — will sup - ply my — need; Je - ho - vah
2. When — I walk — through the shades of — death; Thy — pres - ence

is His name; — In — pas - tures — fresh He
is my stay; — One — word of — Thy sup -

makes me — feed, Be - side the liv - ing stream. —
port - ing — truth, Drives — all my fears a - way. —

He— brings my— wan - d'ring spir - it— back When—
Thy— hand in— sight of all my— foes, Doth—

I for - sake His ways;————— He— leads me— for His
still my— tab - le spread;————— My— cup with— bless - ing

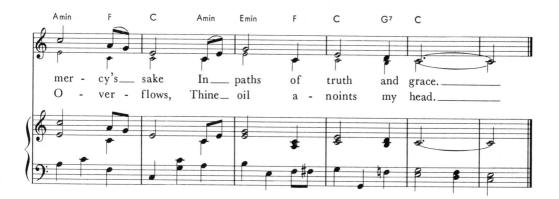

mer - cy's— sake In— paths of truth and grace.—————
O - ver - flows, Thine— oil a - noints my head.—————

Jesus Walked This Lonesome Valley

TRADITIONAL

SPIRITUAL

1. Je - sus walked_____ this lone - some val - ley,_____ He had to
2. We must walk_____ this lone - some val - ley,_____ We have to

walk_____ it by Him - self, Oh,_____ no-bod-y else_____ could walk it
walk_____ it by our - selves, Oh,_____ no-bod-y else_____ can walk it

for Him, He had to walk it by_____ Him - self.
for us, We have to walk it by_____ our - selves.

There Is A Balm In Gilead

TRADITIONAL

SPIRITUAL

There_is a balm in Gil-e-ad, To make the wound-ed whole,___
There_is a balm in Gil-e-ad, To heal the sin-sick soul.

Fine

1. Some-times I feel dis-cour-aged, And think my work in vain,
2. Tho' you can't preach like Pe-ter, And you can't pray like Paul,

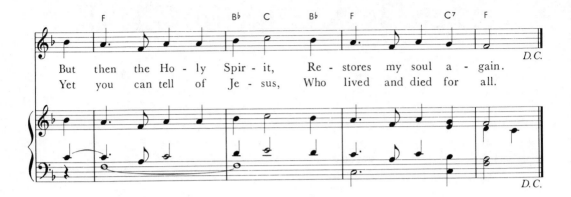

But then the Ho - ly Spir - it, Re - stores my soul a - gain.
Yet you can tell of Je - sus, Who lived and died for all.

D.C.

D.C.

Ev'ry Time I Feel The Spirit

TRADITIONAL

SPIRITUAL

Ev - 'ry time I feel the spir - it mov - ing

in my heart I will pray, Ev - 'ry time I feel the

spir - it mov - ing in my heart I will pray.

1. Up-on the moun-tain when my Lord spoke, Out of His
2. Oh, I have sor-rows, And I have woe,

mouth came fire and smoke; Looked all a-round me, it looked so
heart-ache here be-low; But while God leads me, I'll nev-er

fine, 'Till I asked my Lord if all were mine.
fear, For I am shel-tered ____ by His care.

Let Us Break Bread Together

TRADITIONAL

SPIRITUAL

Let us {break bread / praise God} to-geth-er on our knees,_____ Let us {break bread / praise God} to-

geth - er on our knees,_____ When I fall on my knees, with my

face to the ris - ing sun, Oh Lord, have mer-cy on me._____

Swing Low, Sweet Chariot

TRADITIONAL

SPIRITUAL

Swing low, Sweet char - i - ot,____ com-ing for to car - ry me home,____

Swing____ low, Sweet char - i - ot,____ com-ing for to car - ry me home.____

1. I looked o-ver Jor-dan and what did I see?____
2. If you get____ there____ be - fore____ I do,____ Com-ing for to car-ry me home,____ Just
3. I'm some-times____ up____ and some - times down.____

A
But

band_ of an - gels com-ing af- ter me,___
tell _ my friends I'm com - ing __ too, ___   Com-ing for to car-ry me   home.
still _ my soul feels hea - ven _ bound, ___

D.C.

Were You There?

TRADITIONAL

SPIRITUAL

Were you there when they nailed Him to the tree?_____ Were you
cru - ci - fied my Lord?_____
Laid Him in the tomb?_____

there when they nailed Him to the tree?_____ Oh!_____
cru - ci - fied my Lord?_____
Laid Him in the tomb?_____

Some-times it caus - es me to trem-ble, trem - ble, trem - ble;_____

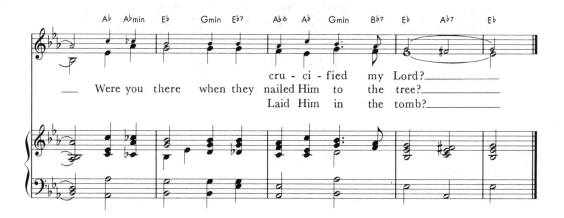

Were you there — when they cru - ci - fied my Lord?_____
Were you there when they nailed Him to the tree?_____
Laid Him in the tomb?_____

He's Got The Whole World
In His Hands

TRADITIONAL

SPIRITUAL

He's got the whole world____ in His hands,____ He's got the
He's got the wind and the rain____ in His hands,____ He's got the

whole world,____ in His hands,__He's got the whole world____
wind and the rain____ in His hands,__He's got the wind and the rain____

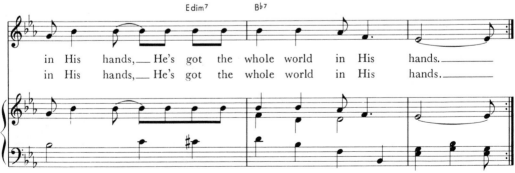

in His hands,__He's got the whole world in His hands.____
in His hands,__He's got the whole world in His hands.____

He's got the lit-tle bit-ty ba-by in His hands,— He's got the
He's got___ you and me___ broth-er, in His hands,— He's got___

lit-tle bit-ty ba-by in His hands,—He's got the lit-tle bit-ty ba-by
you and me,___ broth-er, in His hands,—He's got___ you and me,___ broth-er,

in His hands,— He's got the whole world in His hands.___
in His hands,— He's got the whole world in His hands.___

The Rosary

ETHELBERT NEVIN

Lento, Rerigioso

p—mp

1. The hours I spend with thee, dear heart, Are as a string of pearls to
2. Each hour a pearl, each pearl a pray'r, To still a heart in ab-sence

me; I count them o-ver ev-'ry one a-part, my
wrung: I tell each bead un-to the

ro-sa-ry, my ro-sa-ry! end, And there a cross is hung!

Ah _____ Ah _____

O mem-o-ries that bless and burn!   O bar-ren gain and bit-ter

loss!   I kiss each bead, and strive at last to learn, To kiss the

cross,   Sweet - heart!   To kiss the cross.

Recessional

RUDYARD KIPLING (1865–1936)

REGINALD DE KOVEN (1859–1920)

1. God of our Fathers, known of old, Lord of our far-flung battle line
3. Far called our navies meet away, On dune and headland sinks the fire,

Beneath whose awful hand we hold Dominion over palm and pine;
Lo, all our pomp of yesterday Is one with Nineveh and Tyre!

Lord God of Hosts, be with us yet, Lest we for-get! Lest we for-get!
Judge of the Na - tions, spare us yet, Lest we for-get! Lest we for-get!

Meno mosso

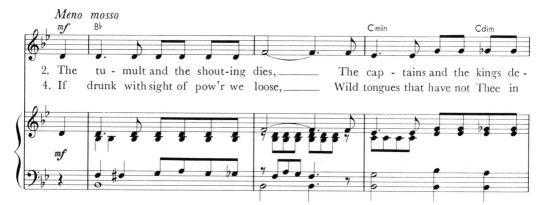

2. The tu - mult and the shout-ing dies,_____ The cap - tains and the kings de -
4. If drunk with sight of pow'r we loose,_____ Wild tongues that have not Thee in

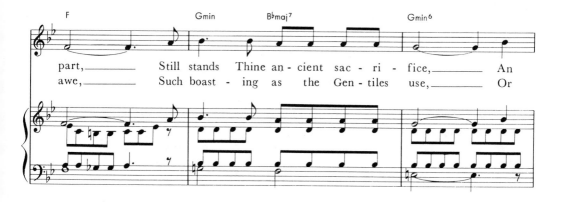

part,_____ Still stands Thine an - cient sac - ri - fice,_____ An
awe,_____ Such boast - ing as the Gen - tiles use,_____ Or

Hum - ble and a con - trite heart,_____
less - er breeds with - out the law,_____
Lord God of Hosts,

Be with us yet, Lest we for-get! Lest we for - get, For-get!

Tempo I

D.S.
5. For hea-then heart that

puts her trust In reek-ing tube and i - ron shard All val-iant dust that builds on dust, And guar-ding, calls not Thee to guard For fran-tic boast and fool - ish word, Thy mer-cy on Thy peo - ple Lord! A - men.

The Holy City

F. E. WEATHERLY

STEPHEN ADAMS

Andante Moderato

1. Last night I lay a - sleep - ing, There came a dream so fair, I stood in old Je - ru - sa - lem, Be - side the tem - ple there: I heard the chil - dren sing - ing, And

2. And then me - thought my dream was changed, The streets no long - er rang, Hushed were the glad Ho - san - nas, The lit - tle chil - dren sang, The sun grew dark with mys - ter - y, The

ev - er   as   they sang,   Me - thought the voice of an - gels from
morn was cold   and chill,   As the shad - ow of   a cross a - rose up -

heav'n   in   an - swer   rang,   Me - thought   the   voice   of
on   a   lone - ly   hill,   As the shad - ow   of   a

an   -   gels   from   heav'n   in   an   -   swer   rang,
cross   a - rose   up   -   on   a   lone - ly   hill.

My Task

MAUDE LOUISE RAY

E. L. ASHFORD

1. To love some-one more dear - ly ev - 'ry day,_____ To
2. To fol - low truth as blind men long for light,_____ To

help a wand -'ring child to find his way,_____ To
Do my best from dawn of day till night,_____ To

Pon - der o'er a no - ble thought, and pray,
keep my heart fit for His ho - ly sight,

And smile when
And an - swer

eve - ning comes, And smile when eve - ning comes,
when He calls, And an - swer when He calls,

This __ is my task.
This __ is my task.

The Lord Bless You And Keep You

PETER C. LUTKIN

you,   be gra-cious,   The Lord   be gra-cious,   gra-cious,   un - to

you, A - - men,   A - - men,   A - -

you,   A - men,   A - men,

men,   A - men,   A - - men,   A - - men.

A - men, _____   A - men,   A - - - - - men.

English

Holy, Holy, Holy

REGINALD HEBER (1783–1826)

JOHN B. DYKES (1823–1876)

1. Ho-ly, ho-ly, ho-ly,— Lord— God Al-might-y,
2. Ho-ly, ho-ly, ho-ly,— all the saints a-dore Thee,

Ear-ly in the morn-ing our song shall rise to Thee.
Cast-ing down their gold-en crowns, a-round the glas-sy sea;

Ho-ly, ho-ly, ho-ly,— mer-ci-ful and might-y!
Cher-u-bim and ser-a-phim,— fall-ing down be-fore Thee,

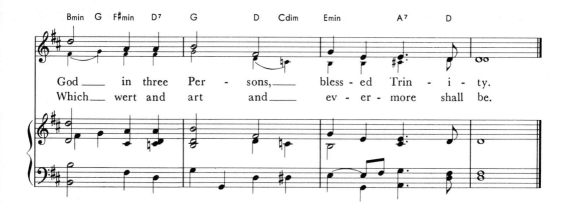

God ___ in three Per - sons, ___ bless - ed Trin - i - ty.
Which ___ wert and art and ___ ev - er - more shall be.

3. Holy, holy, holy! though the darkness hide Thee,
Though the eye of sinful man Thy glory may not see;
Only Thou art holy, there is none beside Thee,
Perfect in power, in love, and purity.

4. Holy, holy, holy! Lord God Almighty!
All Thy works shall praise Thy Name, in earth and sky, and sea;
Holy, holy, holy, merciful and mighty!
God in Three Persons, blessed Trinity!

Praise, My Soul, The King Of Heaven

HENRY F. LYTE (1793–1847)

HENRY SMART (1813–1819)

1. Praise, my soul, the King of heav-en, To His feet thy trib-ute bring;
2. Fa-ther like, He tends and spares us; Well our fee-ble frame He knows;
3. An-gels in the height a-dore Him; Ye be-hold Him face to face;

Ran-somed, healed, re-stored for-giv-en, Ev-er-more His praises sing;
In His hands He gent-ly bears us, Res-cues us from all our foes;
Saints tri-um-phant bow be-fore Him, Gath-ered in from ev-'ry race;

Praise the ev-er-las-ting King.
Al-le-lu-ia, Al-le-lu-ia! Wide-ly yet His mer-cy flows.
Praise with us the God of grace.

O God, Our Help In Ages Past

Based on Psalm 90

ISAAC WATTS (1674–1748)

ATTRIB. TO WILLIAM CROFT (1678–1727)

1. O God, our help in a-ges past, Our hope for years to come,
2. Un-der the shad-ow of Thy Throne, Still may we dwell se-cure;

Our shel-ter from the storm-y blast, And our e-ter-nal home!
Suf-fi-cient is Thine arm a-lone, And our de-fense is sure.

3. Before the hills in order stood,
   Or earth received her frame,
   From everlasting Thou art God,
   To endless years the same.

4. O God, our help in ages past,
   Our hope for years to come;
   Be Thou our guide while life shall last,
   And our eternal home!

Faith Of Our Fathers

HENRI F. HEMY (1818–1888)

FREDERICK W. FABER (1814–1863)

ADAPTED BY JAMES G. WALTON (1821–1905)

1. Faith of our fa - thers! liv - ing still,
2. Faith of our fa - thers! we will strive,
3. Faith of our fa - thers! we will love,

In spite of dun - geon, fire and sword, O how our
To win all na - tions un - to Thee, And through the
Both friend and foe in all our strife, And preach Thee,

hearts beat high with joy When e'er we hear that
truth that comes from God Man kind shall then be
too, as love knows how By kind - ly words and

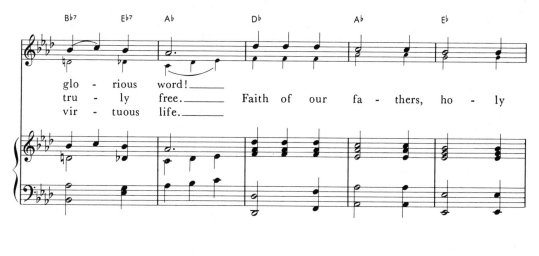

glo - rious word!_____
tru - ly free._____ Faith of our fa - thers, ho - ly
vir - tuous life._____

faith!   We will be true   to   Thee   till   death.

Eternal Father Strong To Save

WILLIAM WHITING (1825–1878)

JOHN B. DYKES (1823–1876)

1. E - ter - nal Fa - ther, strong to save, Whose arm hath bound the rest - less wave,
2. O Trin - i - ty of love and power, Our breth - ren shield in dan-ger's hour;

Who bidd'st the might - y o - cean deep Its own ap - point - ed lim - its keep:
From rock and tem - pest, fire and foe, Pro - tect them where - so - e'er they go:

O hear us when we cry to Thee, For__ those in per - il on the sea.
Thus ev - er - more shall rise to Thee, Glad__ hymns of praise from land and sea.

All Things Bright And Beautiful

CECIL F. ALEXANDER (1823–1895)

OLD ENGLISH MELODY

REFRAIN
All things bright and beau-ti-ful, All crea-tures great and— small,—
All things wise and won-der-ful: The Lord God made them— all.—

VERSE
Each lit-tle flower that— o-pens, Each lit-tle bird—that sings: He—
The pur-ple-head-ed— moun-tain, The riv-er run-ning by, The—

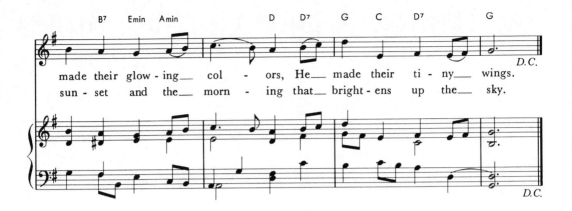

made their glow - ing___ col - ors, He___ made their ti - ny___ wings.
sun - set and the___ morn - ing that___ bright - ens up the___ sky.

D.C.

D.C.

3. The cold wind in the winter,
   The pleasant summer sun,
   The ripe fruits in the garden,
   He made them every one.

4. He gave us eyes to see them,
   And lips that we might tell,
   How great is God Almighty,
   Who has made all things well.

Start with refrain and sing refrain after each verse.

God That Madest Earth And Heaven

REGINALD HEBER (1783–1826)
FREDERICK L. HOSMER (1840–1929)

WELSH MELODY
HARM. BY L. O. EMERSON (1820–1915)

1. God that mad-est earth and heav-en, dark-ness and light,
2. When the con-stant sun re-turn-ing Un-seals our eyes,

Who the day for toil hast giv-en, For rest the night;
May we, born a-new like morn-ing, To la-bor rise;

May Thine an-gel guards de-fend us, Slum-ber sweet thy mer-cy send us;
Gird us for the task that calls us, Let not ease and self en-thrall us,

Ho - ly dreams and hopes at - tend us, This live - long night.
Strong thro' Thee what e'er be - falls us, O God most wise!

Immortal, Invisible

WALTER C. SMITH (1824–1908)

WELSH MELODY

1. Im - mor - tal, in - vis - i - ble, God on - ly wise, In
2. Un - rest - ing, un - hast - ing, and si - lent as light, Nor

light in - ac - ces - si - ble hid from our eyes, Most bless - ed, most glo - rious, the
want - ing, nor wast - ing, Thou rul - est in might; Thy jus - tice like moun - tains high

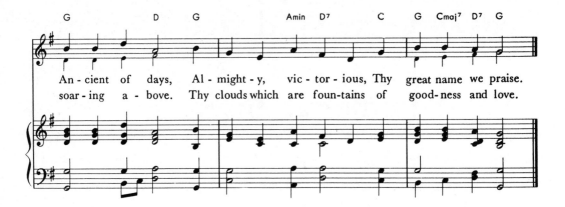

An - cient of days, Al - might - y, vic - tor - ious, Thy great name we praise.
soar - ing a - bove. Thy clouds which are foun-tains of good-ness and love.

3. To all, life Thou givest, to both great and small;
In all life Thou livest, the true life of all;
Thy wisdom so boundless, Thy mercy so free,
Eternal Thy goodness, for naught changeth Thee.

4. Great Father of Glory, pure Father of light,
Thine angels adore Thee, all veiling their sight;
All laud we would render; O help us to see,
'Tis only the splendor of light hideth Thee.

God Of Grace And God Of Glory

HARRY EMERSON FOSDICK (1878–   )

JOHN HUGHES (1873–1932)

1. God of grace and God of glory, On Thy people Pour Thy power; Crown thine ancient Church's story, Bring her bud to glorious flower. Grant us wisdom, Grant us courage,

2. Cure Thy children's warring madness, Bend our pride to Thy control; Shame our wanton, selfish gladness, Rich in things and poor in soul. Grant us wisdom, Grant us courage,

3. Save us from weak resignation To the evils we deplore; Let the search for Thy salvation Be our Glory evermore. Grant us wisdom, Grant us courage,

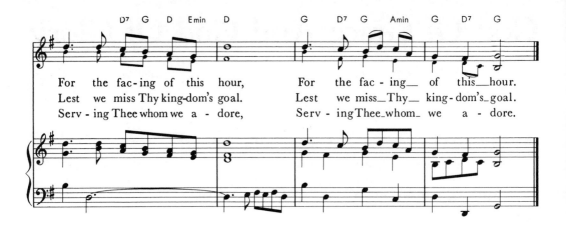

For the fac-ing of this hour, For the fac - ing of this hour.
Lest we miss Thy king-dom's goal. Lest we miss Thy king-dom's goal.
Serv - ing Thee whom we a - dore, Serv - ing Thee whom we a - dore.

Alternate words

1. Guide me, O Thou great Jehovah, Pilgrim through this barren land;
    I am weak but thou art mighty; Hold me with Thy powerful hand;
    Bread of heaven, Bread of heaven,
    Feed me till I want no more, Feed me till I want no more.

2. Open now the crystal fountain, Whence the healing stream doth flow,
    Let the fire and cloudy pillar, Lead me all my journey through;
    Strong Deliverer, strong deliverer,
    Be Thou still my strength and shield, Be Thou still my strength and shield.

3. When I tread the verge of Jordan, Bid my anxious fears subside;
    Death of death, and hell's destruction, Land me safe on Canaan's side.
    Songs of praises, songs of praises,
    I will ever give to Thee, I will ever give to Thee.

The King Of Love My Shepherd Is

HENRY W. BAKER (1821–1877)

JOHN B. DYKES (1823–1876)

1. The King of love my Shep-herd is, whose good-ness fail-eth nev-er;
2. Where streams of liv-ing wa-ter flow, My ran-somed soul He lead-eth,

I noth-ing lack if I am His And He is mine for-ev-er.
And where the ver-dant pas-tures grow, With food ce-les-tial feed-eth.

3. Perverse and foolish oft I strayed,
But yet in love He sought me,
And on His shoulder gently laid,
And home, rejoicing, brought me.

4. In death's dark vale I fear no ill
With Thee, dear Lord, beside me;
Thy rod and staff my comfort still,
Thy cross before to guide me.

5. And so through all the length of days
Thy goodness faileth never;
Good Shepherd, may I sing Thy praise
Within Thy house forever.

O Zion, Haste

MARY A. THOMSON (1834–1923)

JAMES WALCH (1837–1901)

1. O Zi - on, haste, thy mis - sion high ful - fill - ing,
To tell to all the world that God is Light, That He who
made all na - tions is not will - ing One soul should per - ish,

2. Be - hold how man - y thou - sands still are ly - ing,
Bound in the dark - some pris - on - house of sin; With none to
tell them of the Sav - iour's dy - ing, Or of the life He

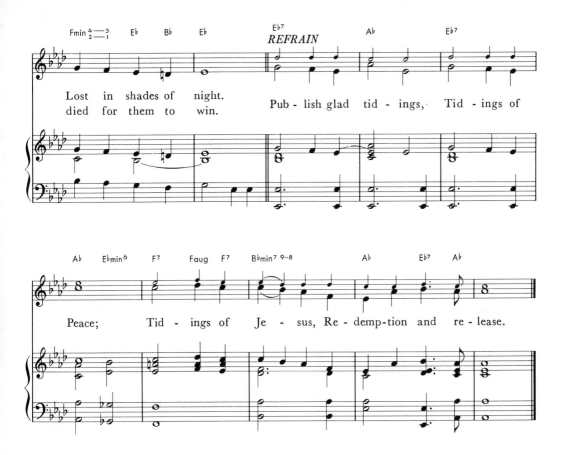

Lost in shades of night.
died for them to win.

REFRAIN

Pub-lish glad tid-ings, Tid-ings of Peace; Tid-ings of Je-sus, Re-demp-tion and re-lease.

3. Proclaim to every people, tongue, and nation
That God, in whom they live and move, is Love;
Tell how He stooped to save His lost creation,
And died on earth that man might live above.
    (*Refrain*)

4. Give of thy sons to bear the message glorious;
Give of thy wealth to speed them on their way;
Pour out thy soul for them in prayer victorious;
O Zion, haste to bring the brighter day.
    (*Refrain*)

Come, Thou Long Expected Jesus

CHARLES WESLEY (1707–1788)

ROWLAND H. PRICHARD (1811–1887)

1. Come, Thou long expected Jesus, Born to set Thy people free; From our fears and sins release us; let us find our rest in Thee, Israel's

2. Born Thy people to deliver, Born a child and yet a King; Born to reign in us forever, Now Thy gracious Kingdom bring. By thine

Strength_ and Con - so - la - tion, Hope of all_ the
own_ e - ter - nal Spir - it, Rule in all_ our

earth_ Thou art;_ Dear_ De - sire_ of Ev - 'ry
hearts_ a - lone;_ By_ thine all_ suf - fi - cient

na - tion, Joy of ev - 'ry_ long - ing heart.
mer - it, Raise us to_ Thy_ glo - rious throne.

Christ The Lord Is Risen Today

CHARLES WESLEY (1707–1788)

FROM *Lyra Davidica*, 1708

1. Christ the Lord is Risen to-day,___ Al - - le - lu - ia!
2. Lives a-gain our glo-rious King,___ Al - - le - lu - ia!

Sons of men and an-gels say,___ Al - - le - lu - ia!
Where, O death, is now thy sting?___ Al - - le - lu - ia!

Raise your joys and___ tri-umphs high, Al - - le - lu - ia!
Once He died our___ souls to save, Al - - le - lu - ia!

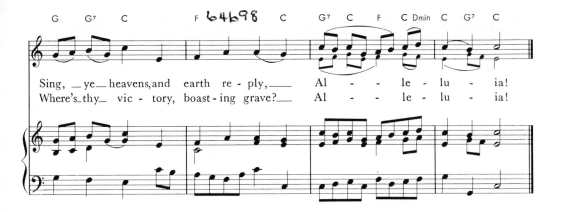

Sing, — ye— heavens, and earth re - ply, ___ Al - - le - lu - ia!
Where's thy— vic - tory, boast - ing grave? ___ Al - - le - lu - ia!

3. Love's redeeming work is done,   Alleluia!
    Fought the fight, the battle won,   "
    Death in vain forbids Him rise,   "
    Christ has opened paradise,   "

4. Soar we now where Christ has led   Alleluia!
    Following our exalted Head,   "
    Made like Him, like Him we rise,   "
    Ours the cross, the grave, the skies,   "

Come Ye Faithful, Raise The Strain

ST. JOHN OF DAMASCUS, 8TH CENTURY
TR. JOHN M. NEALE (1818–1866)

ARTHUR S. SULLIVAN (1842–1900)

1. Come, ye faith - ful, raise the strain Of tri - um - phant glad - ness.
2. 'Tis the spring of souls to - day; Christ hath burst His pris - on,
3. "Al - le - lu - ia!" now we cry To our King Im - mor - tal,

God hath brought His peo - ple forth In - to joy from sad - ness.
From the frost and gloom of death Light and life have ris - en.
Who, tri - um - phant, burst the bars Of the tomb's dark por - tal;

Now re - joice Je - ru - sa - lem, And with true af - fec - tion
All the win - ter of our sins, Long and dark is fly - ing
"Al - le - lu - ia!" with the Son, God the Fa - ther prais - ing;

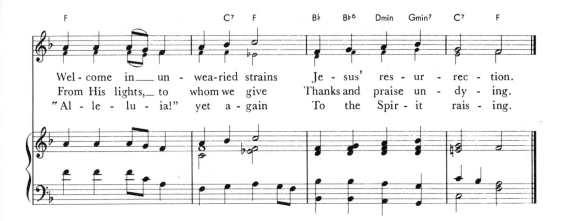

Wel - come in___ un - wea-ried strains Je - sus' res - ur - rec - tion.
From His lights,___ to whom we give Thanks and praise un - dy - ing.
"Al - le - lu - ia!" yet a - gain To the Spir - it rais - ing.

The Church's One Foundation

SAMUEL J. STONE (1839–1900)

SAMUEL S. WESLEY (1810–1876)

1. The Church-'s one foun - da - tion Is Je - sus Christ her Lord;
2. E - lect from ev - 'ry na - tion, Yet one o'er all the earth,

She is His new cre - a - tion By wa - ter and the word:
Her char-ter of sal - va - tion, One Lord, one faith, one birth;

From heav'n He came and sought her To be His ho - ly bride;
One ho - ly Name she bless - es, Par - takes one ho - ly food,

With His own blood He bought her, And for her life He died.
And to one hope she press - es, With ev - 'ry grace en - dued.

3. 'Mid toil and tribulation, And tumult of her war,
   She waits the consummation Of peace forevermore;
   Till, with the vision glorious, Her longing eyes are blest,
   And the great Church victorious, Shall be the Church at rest.

4. Yet she on earth hath union With God the Three in One,
   And mystic sweet communion With those whose rest is won.
   Oh happy one and holy! Lord give us grace that we,
   Like them, the meek and lowly, On high may dwell with Thee.

Alternate words:

1. God is my strong salvation: What foe have I to fear?
   In darkness and temptation, My light, my help, is near:
   Though hosts encamp around me, Firm in the fight I stand;
   What terror can confound me, With God at my right hand?

2. Place on the Lord reliance; My soul, with courage wait;
   His truth be thine affiance, When faint and desolate;
   His might thy heart shall strengthen, His love thy joy increase;
   Mercy thy days shall lengthen, The Lord will give thee peace.

When Morning Gilds The Skies

GERMAN C. 1800
TR. EDWARD CASWALL (1814–1878)

JOSEPH BARNBY (1838–1896)

1. When morn-ing gilds the skies,___ My heart, a - wak - ing cries,___
2. When e'er the sweet church bell___ Peals o - ver hill and dell,___

May Je - sus Christ___ be praised! A - like at work___ and prayer,___
May Je - sus Christ___ be praised! O hark to what___ it sings,___

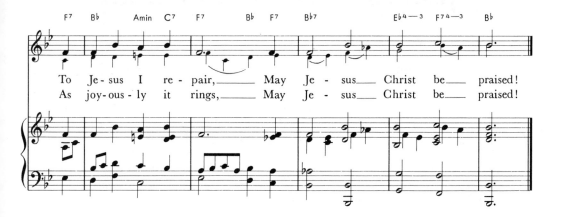

To Je - sus I re - pair,_____ May Je - sus_____ Christ be_____ praised!
As joy-ous-ly it rings,_____ May Je - sus_____ Christ be_____ praised!

3. The night becomes as day, When from the heart we say,
   May Jesus Christ be praised!
   Let all the earth around Ring joyous with the sound,
   May Jesus Christ be praised!

4. Be this, while life is mine, My canticle divine,
   May Jesus Christ be praised!
   Be this th'eternal song Through all the ages long,
   May Jesus Christ be praised!

Jesus, Lover Of My Soul

CHARLES WESLEY (1707–1788)   SIMEON B. MARSH (1798–1875)

1. Je - sus, Lov - er of my soul, Let me to Thy bos - om
2. Oth - er ref - uge have I none, Hangs my help - less soul on
3. Plen - teous grace with Thee is found, Grace to cov - er all my

fly; While the near - er wa - ters roll, While the tem - pest
Thee; Leave, Ah! leave me not a - lone, Still sup - port and
sin; Let the heal - ing streams a - bound, Make and keep me

still is high: Hide me, O__ my Sav - iour, hide,
com - fort me: All my trust__ on thee is stayed,
pure with - in. Thou of life__ the foun - tain art,

Till the storm of life is past; Safe in - to the
All my help from Thee I bring; Cov - er my de -
Free - ly let me take of Thee; Spring Thou up with -

ha - ven guide; O re - ceive my soul at last.
fense - less head With the shad - ow of thy wing.
in my heart, Rise to all e - ter - ni - ty.

Onward, Christian Soldiers

SABINE BARING-GOULD (1834–1924)

ARTHUR S. SULLIVAN (1842–1900)

1. On - ward, Chris - tian sol - diers, March - ing as to war,
2. Like a might - y ar - my Moves the Church of God;

With the cross of Je - sus Go - ing on be - fore.
Broth - ers, we are tread - ing Where the saints have trod;

Christ, the roy - al Mas - ter, leads a - gainst the foe,
We are not di - vid - ed, All one bod - y we,

3. Crowns and thrones may perish, Kingdoms rise and wane,
   But the Church of Jesus Constant will remain;
   Gates of hell can never 'Gainst that Church prevail;
   We have Christ's own promise, And that cannot fail.
   (*Refrain*)

4. Onward, then, ye people, Join our happy throng,
   Blend with ours your voices In the triumph song;
   Glory, laud and honor Unto Christ the King;
   This through countless ages Men and angels sing.
   (*Refrain*)

Now The Day Is Over

SABINE BARING-GOULD (1834–1924)

JOSEPH BARNBY (1838–1896)

1. Now the day is___ o - ver, Night is draw - ing___ nigh,___
2. Je - sus, give the___ wea - ry Calm and sweet re - pose,___

Shad - ows of the eve - ning___ Steal a - cross the sky.
With thy ten - derest bless - ing___ May mine eye - lids close.

3. Grant to little children
    Visions bright of Thee;
    Guard the sailors tossing
    On the deep, blue sea.

4. Comfort every sufferer
    Watching late in pain;
    Those who plan some evil
    From their sins restrain.

All Praise To Thee
My God This Night

THOMAS KEN (1637–1711)

THOMAS TALLIS, *cir.* (1505–1585)

1. All praise to Thee, my God, this night, For all the bless-ings of the light!
2. O may my soul on Thee re-pose; And with sweet sleep mine eye-lids close,

Keep me, O keep me, King of Kings, Be neath thine own Al-might-y wings.
Sleep that may me more vig-'rous make To serve my God when I a-wake.

Abide With Me

HENRY F. LYTE (1793–1847)

WILLIAM H. MONK (1823–1889)

1. A - bide with me, fast falls the e - ven - tide;
2. Swift to its close ebbs out life's lit - tle day;

The dark - ness deep - ens, Lord, with me a - bide!
Earth's joys grow dim, its glo - ries pass a - way;

When oth - er help - ers___ fail and com - forts flee,
Change and de - cay in___ all a - round I see;

| Bb7 | Eb | Bb7 | Eb | G7 | Cmin | Ab6 | Eb | Bb7 | Eb |

Help of the help - less, O a - bide with me.
O Thou who chang - est not, a - bide with me.

3. I need Thy presence every passing hour;
   What but Thy grace can foil the tempter's power?
   Who, like Thyself, my guide and stay can be?
   Thro' cloud and sunshine, Lord, abide with me.

4. Hold Thou Thy cross before my closing eyes;
   Shine through the gloom and point me to the skies;
   Heaven's morning breaks, and earth's vain shadows flee;
   In life, in death, O Lord, abide with me.

Lead, Kindly Light

JOHN HENRY NEWMAN (1801–1890)

JOHN B. DYKES (1823–1876)

1. Lead, kind - ly light, a mid th'en - cir - cling gloom,—
2. I was not ev - er thus, nor prayed that Thou—
3. So long Thy power hath blest me, sure it still—

Lead Thou me on! The night is dark, and I am far from
Shouldst lead me on; I loved to choose and see my path; but
Will lead me on, O'er moor and fen, o'er crag and tor - rent,

home;— Lead Thou me on!— Keep Thou my
now — Lead Thou me on!— I loved the
till — the night is gone.— And with the

feet,_____ I do not ask_____ to_____ see,_____
gar - ish day, and spite_____ of_____ fears,_____
morn _____ those an - gel fac - es_____ smile_____

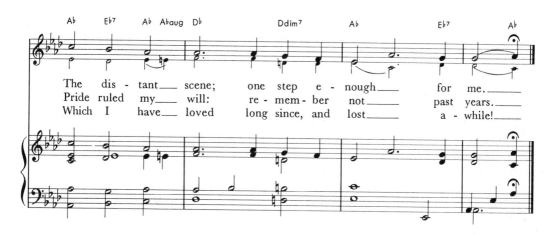

The dis - tant____ scene; one step e - nough____ for me._____
Pride ruled my____ will: re - mem - ber not____ past years._____
Which I have____ loved long since, and lost____ a - while!_____

O Perfect Love

DOROTHY B. GURNEY (1858–1932)

JOSEPH BARNBY (1838–1896)

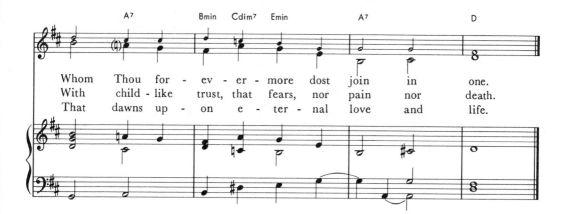

Whom   Thou   for - ev - er - more   dost   join   in   one.
With   child - like   trust, that   fears,   nor   pain   nor   death.
That   dawns   up - on   e - ter - nal   love   and   life.

These Things Shall Be

J. ADDINGTON SYMONDS (1840–1893)

Psalmodia Evangelica, 1789

1. These things shall be: a loft - ier race Than e'er the
World hath known shall rise With flame of free - dom

2. They shall be gen - tle, brave and strong, To spill no
drop of blood, but dare all that may plant man's

In— their— souls And light of knowl - edge— in their eyes.
lord - ship— firm on earth, and fire,— and— sea, and air.

3. Nation with nation, land with land,
   Unarmed shall live as comrades free;
   In every heart and brain shall throb
   The pulse of one fraternity.

4. New arts shall bloom of loftier mold,
   And mightier music thrill the skies,
   And every life shall be a song,
   When all the earth is paradise.

Once To Every Man And Nation

JAMES RUSSELL LOWELL (1819–1891)

WELSH HYMN MELODY

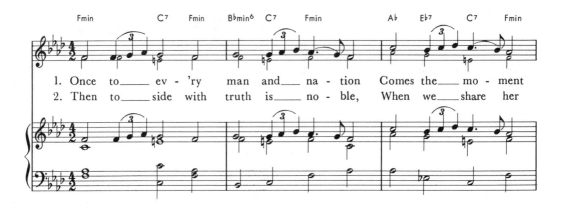

1. Once to____ ev - 'ry man and____ na - tion Comes the____ mo - ment
2. Then to____ side with truth is____ no - ble, When we____ share her

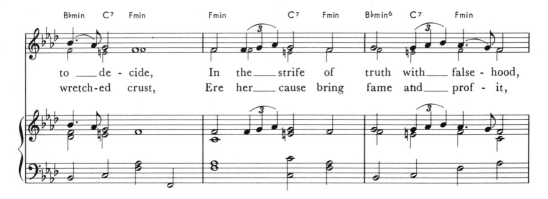

to ___ de - cide, In the____ strife of truth with____ false - hood,
wretch-ed crust, Ere her____ cause bring fame and____ prof - it,

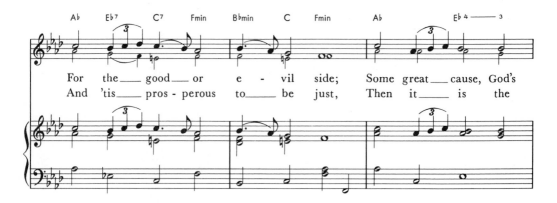

For the___ good ___ or e - vil side; Some great____ cause, God's
And 'tis____ pros - perous to____ be just, Then it____ is the

new Mes - si - ah, Of - fering___ each the bloom or___ blight,
brave man___ choos - es While the___ cow - ard stands a - side,

And the___ choice goes by for - ev - er 'Twixt that___ dark - ness and___ that light.
Till the___ mul - ti - tude make vir___ tue Of the ___faith___they had___ de - nied.

3. By the light of burning martyrs, Christ, Thy bleeding feet we track,
   Toiling up new Calvaries ever With the cross that turns not back;
   New occasions teach new duties, Time makes ancient good uncouth;
   They must upward still and onward, Who would keep abreast of truth.

4. Though the cause of evil prosper, Yet 'tis truth alone is strong:
   Though her portion be the scaffold, And upon the throne be wrong;
   Yet that scaffold sways the future, And, behind the dim unknown,
   Standeth God within the shadow Keeping watch above His own.

Jerusalem The Golden

BERNARD OF CLUNY, 12TH CENTURY
TR. JOHN M. NEALE (1818–1866)

ALEXANDER EWING (1830–1895)

1. Je - ru - sa - lem the gold - en, With milk and hon - ey blest!
2. They stand, those halls of Zi - on, All ju - bi - lant with song,
3. O sweet and bless - ed coun - try, The home of God's e - lect!

Be - neath thy con - tem - pla - tion Sink heart and voice op - pressed:
And bright with many an an - gel, And all the mar - tyr throng;
O sweet and bless - ed coun - try That ea - ger hearts ex - pect!

I know not, oh, I know not, What joys a - wait us There;
The Prince is ev - er in them, The day - light is se - rene;
Je - sus in mer - cy brings us To that dear land of rest;

What ra-dian-cy of glo - ry, What light be-yond com-pare.
The pas-tures of the bless - ed Are decked in glo-rious sheen.
Who art, with God the Fath - er, And Spir-it, ev - er blest.

For All The Saints

WILLIAM W. HOW (1823–1897)

RALPH VAUGHAN WILLIAMS (1872–1958)

1. For all the saints, who from their la - bors rest, Who
2. O blest com - mun - ion, fel - low - ship di - vine!_____

thee_____ by faith be - fore the world con - fessed, Thy
We feeb - ly strug - gle, they in glo - ry shine; Yet

name, O_____ Je - sus, be for - ev - er_____ blest.
all are_____ one in Thee, for all____ are____ Thine.

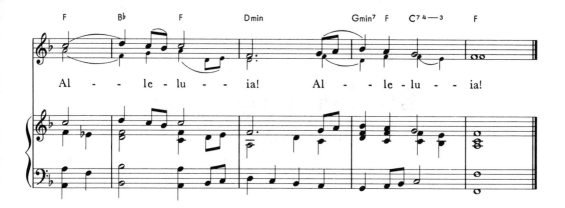

Al - - le - lu - - ia! Al - - le - lu - - ia!

3. And when the strife is fierce, the warfare long,
    Steals on the ear the distant triumph song,
    And hearts are brave again, and arms are strong.
    Alleluia! Alleluia!

4. From earth's wide bounds, from ocean's farthest coast,
    Through gates of pearl streams in the countless host,
    Singing to Father, Son, and Holy Ghost,
    Alleluia! Alleluia!

Brother James' Air

From Psalm 23

JAMES LEITH MACBETH BAIN
(BROTHER JAMES)

1. The Lord's my shep - herd, I'll not want, He makes me down to lie
2. My soul He doth re - store a - gain, And me to walk doth make.

In pas - tures green, He lead - eth me, The qui - et wa - ters by.
With - in the Paths of Bless - ed - ness, E'en for His own Name's sake.

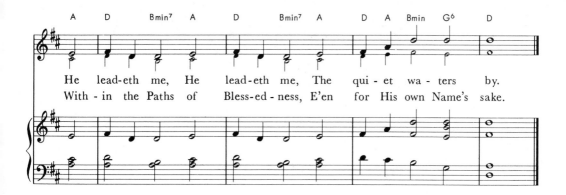

He lead-eth me, He lead-eth me, The qui - et wa - ters by.
With - in the Paths of Bless-ed - ness, E'en for His own Name's sake.

3. Yea, though I pass thro' shadowed vale,
   Yet will I fear no ill:
   For Thou art with me, and Thy Rod
   And Staff me comfort still.
   Thy rod and staff me comfort still,
   Me comfort still.

4. My table Thou hast furnished
   In presence of my foes:
   My head with oil Thou dost anoint,
   And my cup overflows.
   My head Thou dost with oil anoint,
   And my cup overflows.

5. Goodness and mercy all my days
   Will surely follow me;
   And in my Father's heart always
   My dwelling place shall be.
   And in my heart forevermore
   Thy dwelling place shall be.

God So Loved The World

From "The Crucifixion"

JOHN STAINER (1840–1901)

Moderato

God so loved the world,_____ God

so loved the world_____ That He gave His on - ly be -

got - ten Son, That who - so be - liev - eth, be - liev - eth in Him,

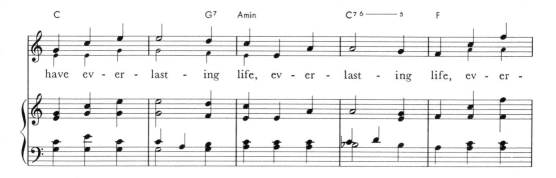

have ev - er - last - ing life, ev - er - last - ing life, ev - er -

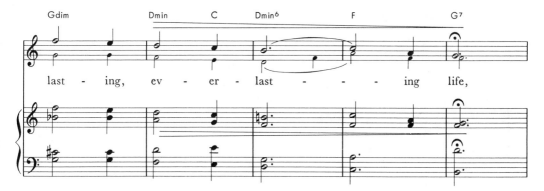

last - ing, ev - er - last - - - ing life,

God so loved the world,_____ God so loved the

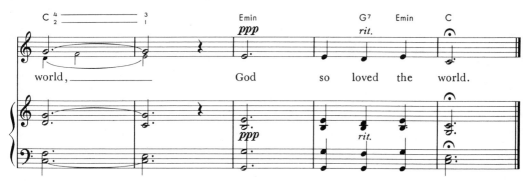

world,_____ God so loved the world.

He Shall Feed His Flock

From "Messiah"

GEORGE F. HANDEL (1685–1759)

He shall—feed His flock like a shep - - herd, And

He—shall—gath - er the lambs—with—His arm, With—His arm.—

He with—His arm.— And

car - ry___them___ in His bo - som, And gent - ly lead___ those___ that

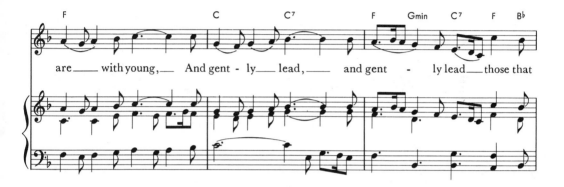

are___ with young,___ And gent - ly___ lead,___ and gent - ly lead___those that

1.

are___ with young.___

2.

And are___ with young.___

Holy Art Thou, Lord God Almighty

GEORGE F. HANDEL (1685–1759)

swells the full har - mo -ny; Bless -ing and glo - ry to the Lamb for- ev - er

more. For wor - thy,___ for wor - thy, wor - thy art___ Thou Let all

na - tions and kin - dreds___ and Peo - ples give___ thanks___ to Thee For - ev - er

more;_____ Give thanks for-ev - er_____ more, Let all na - tions and

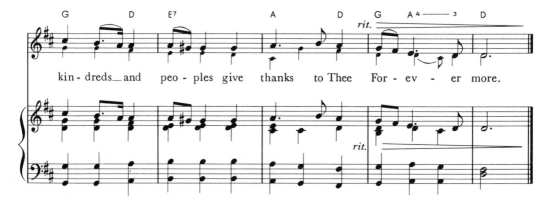

kin - dreds__and peo - ples give thanks to Thee For - ev - er more.

Thanks Be To Thee

GEORGE F. HANDEL (1685–1759)

Lord now ac-cept our thanks,_____

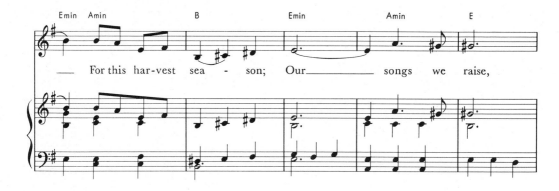

_____ For this har-vest sea - son; Our_____ songs we raise,

Grate - ful-ly we lift our voic-es now,___ and to Thee we give praise.

D.C.

140

German

A Mighty Fortress Is Our God

MARTIN LUTHER (1483–1546)

1. A might-y for-tress is__ our God, A bul-wark nev-er fail - ing;
2. Did we in our__ own strength con-fide Our striv-ing would be los - ing;

Our help-er He__ a-mid__ the flood of mor-tal ills pre-vail - ing:
Were not the right__ Man on__ our side, The Man of God's own choos - ing:

For still our an-cient foe Doth seek to work us woe;
Dost ask who that may be? Christ, Je-sus it is He;

His craft and power are great, And, armed with cru - el hate,
Lord Sa - ba - oth His Name, From age to age the same,

On earth is not his e - - qual.
And he must win the bat - - tle.

3. And tho' this world, with devils filled, Should threaten to undo us,
   We will not fear, for God hath willed His truth to triumph thru' us:
   The Prince of Darkness grim, We tremble not for him, His rage we can endure,
   For lo, his doom is sure, One little word shall fell him.

4. That word above all earthly powers, No thanks to them, abideth;
   The Spirit and the gifts are ours Thru' Him who with us sideth:
   Let goods and kindred go, This mortal life also; The body they may kill:
   God's truth abideth still, His kingdom is forever.

All Glory, Laud And Honor

THEODULPH OF ORLEANS, (*cir.* 760–821)
TR. JOHN M. NEALE (1818–1866)

MELCHIOR TESCHNER (1585–1635)

1. All glo-ry, laud, and hon - or, To Thee, Re - deem - er, King,
2. The com - pa - ny of an - gels Are prais-ing Thee on high,
3. To Thee be - fore Thy Pas - sion They sang their hymns of praise:

To whom the lips of chil - dren made sweet ho - san - nas ring,
And mor - tal men and all things Cre - a - ted make re - ply,
To Thee now high ex - alt - ed, Our mel - o - dy we raise.

Thou art the King of Is - ra - el, Thou Da - vid's roy - al Son,
The peo - ple of the He - brews With palms be - fore Thee went;
Thou didst ac - cept their prais - es, Ac - cept the praise we bring;

Who in the Lord's Name com - est, the King and Bless - ed One.
Our praise and prayer and an - thems Be - fore Thee we pre - sent.
Who in all good de - light - est, Thou good and gra - cious King.

For The Beauty Of The Earth

FOLLIOTT S. PIERPOINT (1835–1917)

CONRAD KOCHER (1786–1872)

For the— beau-ty of the earth, For the glo - ry of the skies,
For the— beau-ty of each hour, Of the day and of the night,

For the— love which from our birth O - ver and a - round us lies,
Hill and— vale and tree and flower, Sun and moon and stars of light:

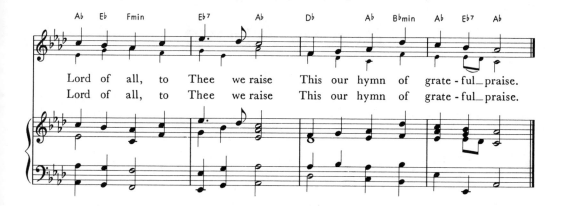

Lord of all, to Thee we raise This our hymn of grate - ful_praise.
Lord of all, to Thee we raise This our hymn of grate - ful_praise.

3. For the joy of human love,
   Brother, sister, parent, child,
   Friends on earth, and friends above;
   For all gentle thoughts and mild;
   Lord of all, to Thee we raise
   This our hymn of grateful praise.

4. For Thyself, best gift divine;
   To our race so freely given;
   For that great, great love of Thine,
   Peace on earth, and joy in heaven:
   Lord of all, to Thee we raise
   This our hymn of grateful praise.

Sing Praise To God Who Reigns Above

JOHANN J. SCHÜTZ (1640–1690)
TR. FRANCES C. COX (1812–1897)

FROM THE *Bohemian Brethren's*
Gesangbuch, 1566

1. Sing praise to God who reigns a - bove, The_____
God of all cre - a - tion, The God of power the
God of love, The_____ God of our sal - va - tion, With

2. What God's al - might - y power hath made, His_____
gra - cious mer - cy_____ keep - eth; By morn - ing glow or
eve - ning shade His_____ watch-ful eye ne'er_____ sleep - eth; With -

heal-ing balm my soul He fills, And ev - ery faith - less mur - mur stills: To___ God all praise and___ glo - ry!

in the king - dom of His might, Lo! all is just, and all is right, To___ God all praise and___ glo - ry!

3. Then all my gladsome way along, I sing aloud Thy praises,
That men may hear the grateful song My voice unwearied raises;
Be joyful in the Lord, my heart, Both soul and body bear your part;
To God all praise and glory.

4. O ye who name Christ's holy name, Give God all praise and glory;
All ye who own His power, proclaim Aloud the wondrous story!
Cast each false idol from His throne, The Lord is God and He alone;
To God all praise and glory.

Glorious Things Of Thee Are Spoken

JOHN NEWTON (1725–1807)

FRANZ JOSEPH HAYDN (1732–1809)

1. Glo - rious things of Thee are spo - ken, Zi - on, Cit - y of our God;
2. See the streams of liv - ing wa - ters, Spring-ing from e - ter - nal love;
3. 'Round each hab - i - ta - tion hov-ering, See the cloud and fire ap - pear.

He, whose word can - not be bro - ken, Formed Thee for His own a - bode;
Well sup - ply Thy sons and daugh-ters, and all fear of want re - move;
For a glo - ry and a cov - ering, show - ing that the Lord is near!

On the rock of a - ges found-ed, What can shake Thy sure re-pose?
Who can faint, while such a riv - er Ev - er flows their thirst t'as-suage?
Glo-rious things of Thee are spo - ken, Zi - on Cit - y of our God;

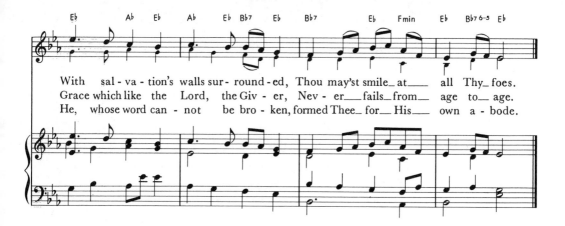

With sal-va-tion's walls sur-round-ed, Thou may'st smile_ at___ all Thy_ foes.
Grace which like the Lord, the Giv - er, Nev - er___ fails_ from__ age to__ age.
He, whose word can - not be bro - ken, formed Thee_ for__ His__ own a - bode.

Alternate words:

From the Foundling Hospital Collection, 1796

1. Praise the Lord, ye heavens adore Him;
    Praise Him angels in the height;
    Sun and moon, rejoice before Him,
    Praise Him all ye stars of light.
    Praise the Lord, for He hath spoken;
    Worlds His mighty voice obeyed;
    Laws which never shall be broken
    For their guidance He hath made.

2. Praise the Lord, for He is glorious;
    Never shall His promise fail;
    God hath made His saints victorious;
    Sin and death shall not prevail.
    Praise the God of our salvation!
    Hosts on high His power proclaim;
    Heaven and earth, and all creation,
    Laud and magnify His Name.

Praise To The Lord

Based on Psalms 103 and 150

JOACHIM NEANDER (1650–1680)

TR. CATHERINE WINKWORTH (1829–1878)

FROM *Praxis Pietatis Melica*, 1668

1. Praise to the Lord, the Al - might - y, the King of cre - a - tion!
2. Praise to the Lord, who o'er all things so won-drous-ly Reign - eth,
3. Praise to the Lord, who doth pros - per Thy work and de - fend Thee;

O my soul, praise Him, for He is Thy health and sal - va - tion!
Shield-eth thee un - der His wings, yea, so gent - ly sus - tain - eth!
sure - ly His good - ness and mer - cy here dai - ly at - tend Thee!

All ye who hear, Now to His tem - ple draw near;
Hast thou not seen How thy de - sires e'er have been
Pon - der a - new What the Al - might - y can do,

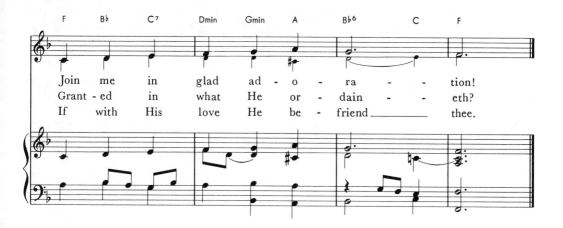

Join me in glad ad - o - ra - - tion!
Grant - ed in what He or - dain - - eth?
If with His love He be - friend _____ thee.

The Spacious Firmament On High

JOSEPH ADDISON (1672–1719)

FRANZ JOSEPH HAYDN (1732–1809)

1. The spa - cious firm - a - ment on high, With all the blue e - the - real sky, And span - gled heav'ns, a shin - ing frame, Their great O - rig - in - al pro - claim.

2. Soon as the eve - ning shades pre - vail, The moon takes up the won - drous tale, And night - ly, to the lis - t'ning earth, re - peats the sto - ry of her birth;

3. What tho' in sol - emn si - lence all Move round the dark ter - res - tial ball? What tho' no re - al voice nor sound A - mid the ra - diant orbs be found?

The'un-wea - ried sun, from day to day, Does his_____ Cre -
While all the stars that round her burn, And all_____ the
In rea - son's ear they all re - joice, And ut - ter

a - tor's power_____ dis - play, And pub - lish - es to
plan - ets in_____ their turn, Con - firm the tid - ings
forth_____ a glo - rious voice; For - ev - er sing - ing,

ev - ery land The work_____ of an_____ al - might - y_____ hand.
as they roll, And spread_____ the truth_____ from pole to_____ pole.
As they shine, "The hand_____ that made_____ us is di - vine."

O Worship The King

Based on Psalm 104

ROBERT GRANT (1779–1838)   JOHANN M. HAYDN (1737–1806)

1. O wor-ship the King, all glo-rious a-bove, O grate-ful-ly sing His power_and His love; our Shield and De-fend-er, the An-cient of Days, Pa-vil-ioned in splen-dor, and gird-ed with praise.

2. Thy boun-ti-ful care what tongue can re-cite? It breathes in the air, It shines_in the light, It streams from the hills, it de-scends to the plain, And sweet-ly dis-tills in the dew_and the rain.

3. Frail chil-dren of dust, and fee-ble as frail, In Thee do we trust, nor find_Thee to fail; Thy mer-cies how ten-der, how firm to the end, Our Ma-ker, De-fend-er, Re-deem-er and Friend!

Joyful, Joyful, We Adore Thee

HENRY VAN DYKE (1852–1933)

LUDWIG VAN BEETHOVEN (1772–1827)

1. Joy-ful, joy-ful, we a - dore Thee, God of glo - ry, Lord of love;
2. All Thy works with joy sur - round Thee, earth and heaven re - flect Thy rays,

Hearts un - fold like flow'rs be - fore Thee, Open-ing to the sun a - bove.
Stars and an - gels sing a - round Thee, Cen - ter of un - bro - ken praise;

Melt the clouds of sin and sad - ness: Drive the dark of doubt a - way;
Field and for - est, vale and moun-tain, Flow-ery mead - ow, flash - ing sea,

Giv - er of im - mor - tal glad - ness, Fill us with the light of day!
Chant-ing bird and flow - ing foun - tain, Call us to re - joice in Thee.

Alternate words: **Sing With All The Sons Of Glory**

WILLIAM J. IRONS (1812-1883)

1. Sing with all the sons of glory,
    Sing the resurrection song!
    Death and sorrow, earth's dark story,
    To the former days belong;
    All around the clouds are breaking,
    Soon the storms of time shall cease,
    In God's likeness, man awaking,
    Knows the everlasting peace.

2. Life eternal! O what wonders
    Crowd on faith; what joy unknown,
    When, amidst earth's closing thunders,
    Saints shall stand before the throne!
    O to enter that bright portal,
    See the glowing firmament,
    Know with Thee, O God Immortal,
    "Jesus Christ whom Thou hast sent!"

Holy God, We Praise Thy Name

GERMAN 18TH CENTURY

TR. CLARENCE WALWORTH (1820–1900)

Allgemeines Katholisches Gesangbuch, VIENNA, 1774

1. Ho - ly God,___ we praise___ Thy name! Lord of all___ we bow___ be - fore Thee; All on earth___ Thy scep - tre claim, All in heav'n___ a - bove___ a - dore Thee:

2. Hark! the loud___ ce - les - tial hymn An - gel choirs___ a - bove___ are rais - ing; Cher - u - bim___ and ser - a - phim In un - ceas - ing cho - rus prais - ing:

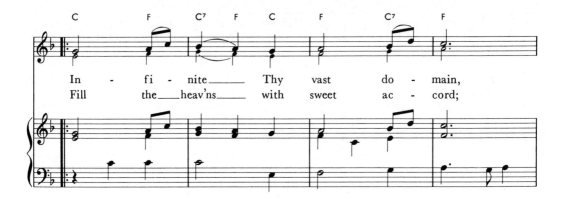

In - fi - nite_____ Thy vast do - main,
Fill the___heav'ns___ with sweet ac - cord;

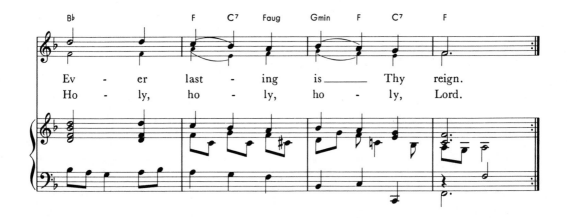

Ev - er last - ing is_____ Thy reign.
Ho - ly, ho - ly, ho - ly, Lord.

We Gather Together

NETHERLAND FOLK SONG, 1625
ARR. BY EDWARD KREMSER (1838–1914)

ANONYMOUS

1. We gath - er to - geth - er to ask the Lord's bless - ing;
2. Be - side us to guide us, our God with us join - ing,
3. We all do ex - tol Thee, Thou Lead - er tri - um - phant,

He chas - tens and has - tens His will to make known;
Or - dain - ing, main - tain - ing His King - dom di - vine;
And pray that Thou still our De - fend - er wilt be.

The wick - ed op - press - ing now cease from dis - tress - ing,
So from the be - gin - ning the fight we were win - ning;
Let Thy con - gre - ga - tion es - cape trib - u - la - tion!

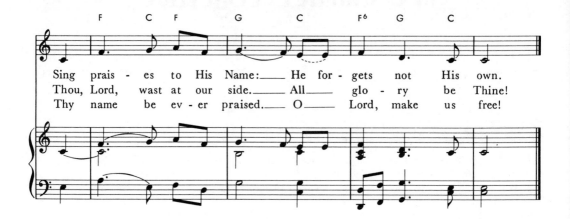

Sing prais - es to His Name:⎯ He for - gets not His own.
Thou, Lord, wast at our side.⎯ All⎯ glo - ry be Thine!
Thy name be ev - er praised.⎯ O⎯ Lord, make us free!

Fairest Lord Jesus

FROM *Schlesische Volksglieder* (1842)

ARR. BY RICHARD S. WILLIS (1819–1900)

GERMAN 17TH CENTURY

(Descant on ah or on words ad lib.)

1. Fair - est Lord Je - sus, Ru - ler of all na - ture, O Thou of
2. Fair are the mead - ows, Fair - er still the wood - lands, Robed in the
3. Fair is the sun - shine, Fair - er still the moon - light, and all the

God and__ man the Son, Thee will I cher - ish,
bloom - ing__ garb of spring: Je - sus is fair - er,
twink - ling__ star - ry host: Je - sus shines bright - er,

Thee will I hon - or, Thee my soul's Glo - ry, Joy and Crown.
Je - sus is pur - er, Who makes the woe - ful heart to sing.
Je - sus shines pur - er Than all the an - gels heaven can boast.

Ah, Holy Jesus

JOHANN HEERMANN (1585–1647)
TR. ROBERT BRIDGES (1844–1930)

JOHANN CRÜGER (1598–1662)

1. Ah, ho-ly Je - sus, how hast Thou of - fend - ed,
2. For me, kind Je - sus, was Thy In - car - na - tion,
3. There - fore, kind Je - sus, since I can - not pay Thee,

That man to judge Thee hath in hate pre - tend - ed? By foes de -
Thy mor - tal sor - row, and Thy life's ob - la - tion; Thy death of
I do a - dore Thee, and will ev - er pray Thee, Think on Thy

rid - ed, by Thine own re - jec - ted, O most af - flict - ed.
an - guish, and Thy bit - ter Pas - sion, For my sal - va - tion.
pit - y and Thy love un - swerv - ing, Not my de - serv - ing.

O Come And Mourn

FREDERICK W. FABER (1814–1863)   GERMAN, 1631

1. O come and mourn with me a-while! See, Ma-ry calls us
2. Have we no tears to shed for Him, While sol-diers scoff and
3. O love of God! O sin of man! In this dread act your

to her side; O come and let us mourn with her;
foes de-ride; Ah! look how pa-tient-ly He hangs;
strength is tried; And vic-to-ry re-mains with love;

REFRAIN

Je - sus, our love, is cru-ci-fied, Je - sus, our love, is cru-ci-fied.

O Sacred Head Now Wounded

ASCRIBED TO BERNARD OF CLAIRVAUX (1091–1153)
GERMAN TR. PAUL GERHARDT (1607–1676)
ENG. TR. JAMES W. ALEXANDER (1804–1859)

HANS L. HASSLER (1564–1612)
HARM. BY JOHANN S. BACH (1685–1750)

1. O sa-cred Head, now wound-ed, With grief and shame weighed down,
2. What Thou, my Lord, hast suf-fered Was all for sin-ners' gain:
3. What lan-guage shall I bor-row To thank Thee, dear-est Friend,

Now scorn-ful-ly sur-round-ed, With thorns, Thine on-ly crown;
Mine, mine was the trans-gres-sion, But Thine the dead-ly pain.
For this Thy dy-ing sor-row, Thy pit-y with-out end?

How pale Thou art with an-guish, With sore a-buse and scorn!
Lo, here I fall, my Sav-iour! 'Tis I de-serve Thy place;
O make me Thine for-ev-er; And should I faint-ing be,

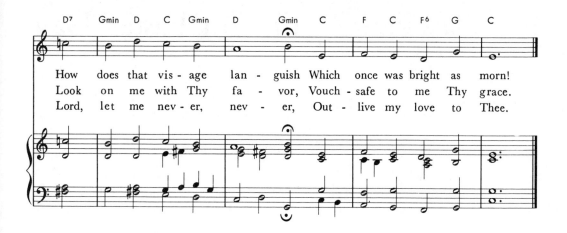

How does that vis - age lan - guish Which once was bright as morn!
Look on me with Thy fa - vor, Vouch - safe to me Thy grace.
Lord, let me nev - er, nev - er, Out - live my love to Thee.

Joy Dawned Again On Easter Day

LATIN 5TH CENTURY
TR. JOHN M. NEALE (1818–1866)

MELODY FROM *Geistliche Kirchengesänge*, COLOGNE (1623)

1. Joy dawned a-gain on Eas-ter-Day, The sun shone out with fair-er
2. O Je-sus, King of gen-tle-ness, Do Thou our in-most hearts pos-

ray, Al - le - lu – ia, Al - le - lu – ia! When
sess, And

to their long-ing eyes re - stored, Th'A - pos-tles saw their ris - en
we to Thee will ev - er raise The trib-ute of our grate-ful

Lord. / praise.
Al - le - lu - ia, Al - le - lu - ia, Al - le -
lu - ia, Al - le - lu - ia, Al - le - lu - - ia!

3. Jesus who art the Lord of all,
   In this our Easter festival, Alleluia,
   From every weapon death can wield
   Thine own redeemed, Thy people, shield. Alleluia.

4. All praise, O risen Lord, we give
   To Thee, who, dead, again dost live; Alleluia,
   To God the Father equal praise,
   And God the Holy Ghost, we raise. Alleluia.

Alternate words: **All Creatures Of Our God And King**

ST. FRANCIS OF ASSISI (1182–1226)
TR. WILLIAM H. DRAPER (1855–1933)

1. All creatures of our God and King,
   Lift up your voice and with us sing, Alleluia,
   Thou burning sun with golden beam
   Thou silver moon with softer gleam,
   O praise Him, O praise Him! Alleluia!

2. Thou rushing wind that art so strong,
   Ye clouds that sail in heaven along, O praise Him, Alleluia,
   Thou rising morn, in praise rejoice,
   Ye lights of evening find a voice!
   O praise Him, O praise Him! Alleluia!

3. Thou flowing water, pure and clear,
   Make music for Thy Lord to hear, Alleluia,
   Thou fire so masterful and bright,
   Thou givest man both warmth and light!
   O praise Him, O praise Him! Alleluia!

4. Let all things their Creator bless,
   And worship Him in humbleness, O praise Him! Alleluia!
   Praise, praise the Father, praise the Son,
   And praise the Spirit, Three in One!
   O praise Him, O praise Him! Alleluia!

169

Now Thank We All Our God

MARTIN RINKART (1586–1649)
TR. CATHERINE WINKWORTH (1829–1878)

JOHANN CRÜGER (1598–1662)

1. Now thank we all our God With heart and hands and voic - es,
2. O may this boun - teous God Through all our life be near us,
3. All praise and thanks to God The Fa - ther now be giv - en,

Who won - drous things hath done, In whom His world re - joic - es;
With ev - er joy - ful hearts And bless - ed peace to cheer us;
The Son, and Him who reigns With Them in high - est hea - ven,

Who from our moth - ers' arms, Hath blessed us on our way,
And keep us in His grace, And guide us when per - plexed,
The one e - ter - nal God, Whom earth and heav'n a - dore,

With count-less gifts of love, and still is ours to - day.
And free us from all ills in this world and the next.
For thus it was, is now, and shall be ev - er - more.

Jesu, Joy Of Man's Desiring

JOHANN S. BACH (1685–1750)

Je - su, Joy of man's de - sir - ing, Ho - ly

wis - dom, Love_____ most bright; Drawn by Thee, our

souls, as - pir - ing, soar to un - cre - a - ted

light. Word of God our flesh that fash-ioned With the fire___ of life___ im-pas-sioned, Striv - ing still to truth un - known, Soar - ing, dy - ing 'round___ Thy throne.

Jesus, Priceless Treasure

JOHANN FRANCK (1618–1677)
TR. CATHERINE WINKWORTH (1829–1878)
ALT. G.K.E.

JOHANN CRÜGER (1598–1662)
HARM. BY JOHANN S. BACH, 1723 [G.K.E.]

1. Je - sus, price - less treas - ure, Source of pur - est pleas - ure,
2. Hence, with earth - ly treas - ure! Thou art all my pleas - ure,
3. Hence, all fear and sad - ness! For the Lord of glad - ness,

Tru - est friend art Thou to me; Ah how long I've pant - ed,
Tru - est Je - sus, all my choice; Hence, thou emp - ty glo - ry!
Bless-ed Je - sus, en - ters in; Those who love the Fa - ther,

And my heart hath faint - ed, Thirst-ing Lord, for Thee.
Naught to me thy sto - ry, Told with tempt - ing voice;
Though the storms may gath - er, Still have peace with - in;

Thine I am, O spot - less Lamb! I will suf - fer naught to__ hide
Pain or loss, or shame, or cross, shall not from my Sav - iour__ move
Yea, what-e'er I here must bear, Thou art still my pur - est__ pleas -

Thee, Naught I ask be - side Thee.
me, Since He deigns to__ love me.
ure, Je - sus, price - less__ treas - ure.

Come, Blessed Death

JOHANN S. BACH (1685–1750)

1. Come, bless - ed____ death, Sweet, sooth - ing____ rest! Guide thou my____ steps home - ward turn - - ing, Leav - ing the world____ and____ its____ yearn - - ing. Thy peace shall____ in me____ dwell,

2. Come, blest re - pose, My eye - lids____ close; Turn - eth my____ hope now____ to heav - - en, As is Thy true____ prom - ise____ giv - - en. Sol - ace I____ seek in____ Thee,

And __ mor - tal fears_____ dis - pel._____ Calm be__ my__
Come__ now__ and set_____ me__ free;_____ Thus shall__ I__

Fail - - ing__ breath, Come__ bless - ed__ death.
e'er_____ be__ blest, Sweet,__ sooth - ing__ rest!

Wake, Awake, For Night Is Flying

JOHANN S. BACH (1685–1750)

1. Wake, a - wake, for night is fly - ing, The watch - men on the heights are cry - ing, A - wake, Je - ru - se - lem at last. The Bride - groom
2. Mid - night hears the wel - come voic - es, And at the thrill - ing cry re - joic - es: Come forth, ye vir - gins, night is past.

comes; a - wake, Your__ lamps with glad - ness take;

Al - le - lu - ia, And for His mar - riage__

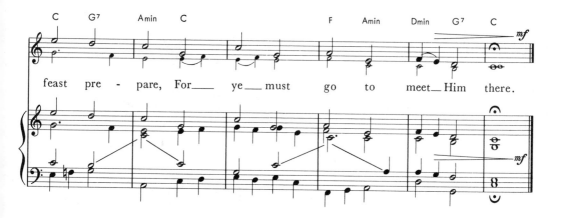

feast pre - pare, For__ ye__ must go to meet__ Him there.

O Saviour, Hear Me

C. W. VON GLUCK (1714–1787)

1. O Sav - iour hear me I im - plore Thee,
2. Thou canst sus - tain And Thou re - store me,
3. Lord, I long for Thy sal - va - tion,

In Thee a - lone can peace be found.
What - e'er the cares that hov - er round.
And would fain at - tain the prize.

Fine

REFRAIN
Hear my sup - pli - ca - tion,

Turn_____ on__ me_____ Thy lov - ing__ eyes,_____ O

Turn_____ on me_____ Thy lov - ing eyes.

D.C.

D.C.

Jesu, Word Of God Incarnate

WOLFGANG A. MOZART (1756–1791)

Je - su,— word— of God— In—

car - nate, Of the Vir - gin Ma - ry born,

On the cross— Thy sa - cred Bod - y, For us—

men, with nails___ was torn.

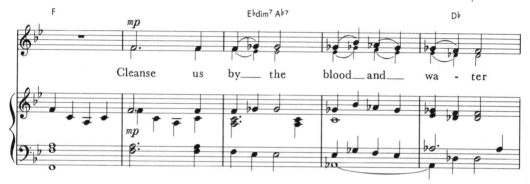

Cleanse us by___ the blood___ and___ wa - ter

Stream - ing from___ Thy___ pierc - ed side   Feed   us

with___ Thy___ Bod - y bro - ken,___ Now,_____ and in death's

Ave Maria

FRANZ SCHUBERT (1797–1828)

Poco lento

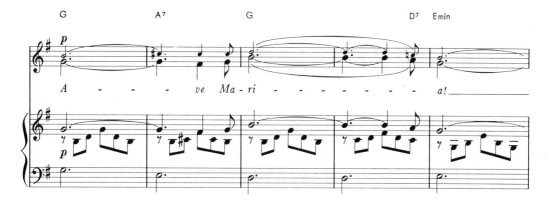

186

tu in mu - li - e - ri - bus,_____ et be - - ne

dic - - - - - tus,_____ et be - - ne

dic - tus fruc - tus ven - tris,_____ ven - tris tu - i,

Je - - - sus._____ A - -

- - ve Ma - ri - - - - - - a!

But The Lord Is Mindful Of His Own

From "St. Paul"

FELIX MENDELSSOHN (1809–1847)

But the Lord is mind-ful of His own,___ He___ re - mem-bers His chil -

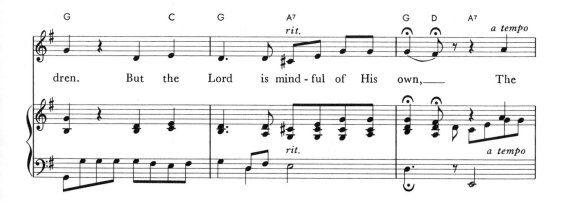

dren. But the Lord is mind-ful of His own,___ The

Lord re-mem-bers His chil - dren, re - mem - - bers His

chil - dren.   Bow down be-fore Him, ye

might - y,   For   the Lord is   near   us,   Bow down be-fore Him, ye

might - y,   For   the Lord is   near   us.   Yea, the

Lord is mind - ful of His own,___ He___ re - mem - bers His chil - -

dren. Bow down be - fore Him, ye might - y, For the

Lord is near us.

O Rest In The Lord

From Psalm 37

FELIX MENDELSSOHN (1809–1847)

O rest in the Lord, wait pa-tient-ly for Him, and He shall give thee thy heart's de-sires;___ O rest___ in the Lord, wait pa-tient-ly for Him, and He___ shall___ give thee thy heart's_ de-sires,___ and He shall

give thee thy heart's___ de - sires. Com-mit thy way un - to Him,___ and trust in

Him; com-mit thy way un - to Him,___ and trust in Him, and fret___ not thy -

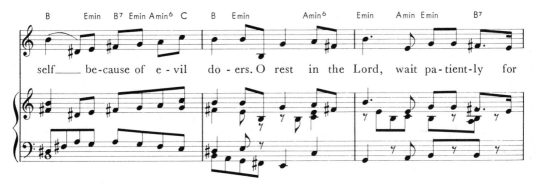

self___ be-cause of e - vil do - ers. O rest in the Lord, wait pa-tient-ly for

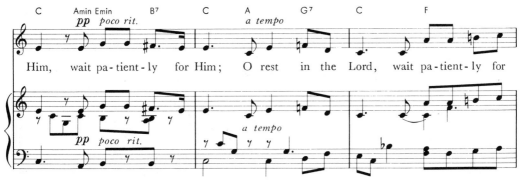

Him, wait pa-tient-ly for Him; O rest in the Lord, wait pa-tient-ly for

Cast Thy Burden Upon The Lord

FELIX MENDELSSOHN (1809–1847)

Cast thy___ bur-den up-on the Lord, And He will sus-

tain___ thee, He___ nev-er will suf-fer the right-eous to fall, He is at thy

right___ hand. Thy mer-cy, Lord, is great; and far a-bove the___

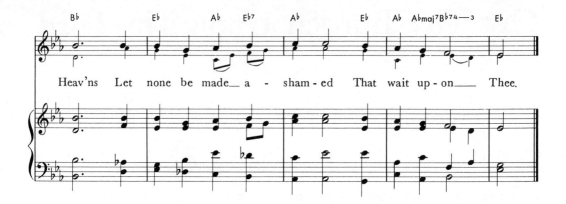

Heav'ns Let none be made— a - sham - ed That wait up - on—— Thee.

Children's Prayer

From "Hansel and Gretel"

ENGELBERT HUMPERDINCK (1854–1921)

When at night I go to sleep, Four-teen an-gels watch do__ keep,__

Two my head are guard - ing, Two my feet are guid - ing,

Two are at__ my right__ hand, Two are at my left__ hand,

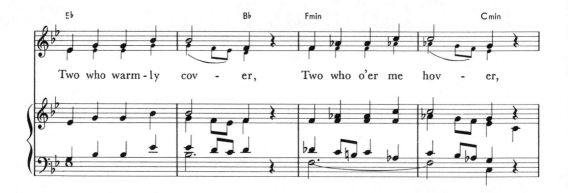

Two who warm-ly cov - er, Two who o'er me hov - er,

Two to whom is giv - en To guide my steps to Heav - - en.

Italian

Come, Thou Almighty King

ANONYMOUS

FELICE DE GIARDINI (1716–1796)

1. Come, Thou Al - might - y King, Help us Thy Name___ to sing,
2. Come, Thou in - car - nate Word, Gird on Thy might - y sword,

Help us to praise! Fa - ther all glo - ri - ous, o'er all vic -
Our prayer at - tend: Come, and Thy peo - ple bless, And give Thy

to - ri - ous, Come, and reign o - ver us, An - cient of Days!
word suc-cess; Spir - it of ho - li - ness, On us de - scend!

3. Come, Holy Comforter, Thy sacred witness bear,
In this glad hour:
Thou who almighty are, Now rule in every heart,
And ne'er from us depart,
Spirit of power!

4. To Thee, great One in Three, Eternal praises be,
Hence, evermore:
Thy sovereign majesty May we in glory see,
And to eternity
Love and adore!

The Strife Is O'er

AUTHORSHIP UNCERTAIN
TR. FRANCIS POTT (1832–1909)

GIOVANNI P. DA PALESTRINA (1524–1594)

Al - le - lu - ia! Al - le - lu - ia! Al - le - lu

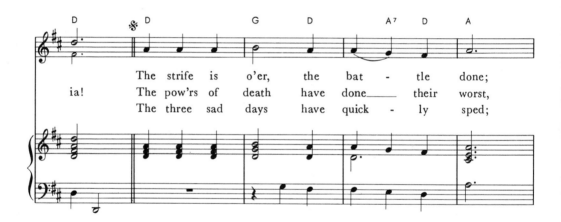

ia!   The strife is o'er, the bat - tle done;
   The pow'rs of death have done their worst,
   The three sad days have quick - ly sped;

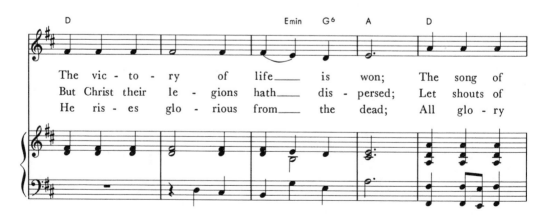

The vic - to - ry of life is won; The song of
But Christ their le - gions hath dis - persed; Let shouts of
He ris - es glo - rious from the dead; All glo - ry

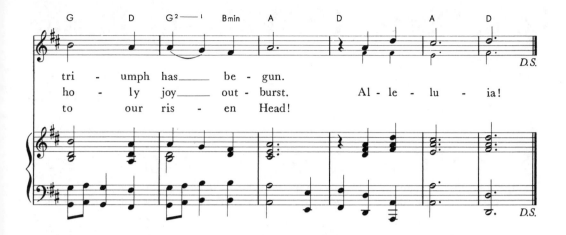

tri - umph has____ be - gun.
ho - ly joy____ out - burst.   Al - le - lu - ia!
to   our ris - en Head!

Lord, Dismiss Us With Thy Blessing

JOHN FAWCETT (1740-1817)

SICILIAN MELODY

1. Lord, dis-miss us with Thy bless-ing, Fill our hearts with joy and peace;
2. Thanks we give and ad-o-ra-tion, For Thy gos-pel's joy-ful sound,

Let us each Thy love pos-sess-ing, Tri-umph in re-deem-ing grace:
May the fruits of Thy sal-va-tion, In our hearts and lives a-bound;

Oh, re-fresh us, Oh, re-fresh us, Trav-'ling thro' this wil-der-ness.
Ev-er faith-ful, ev-er faith-ful To the truth may we be found.

204

French

All People That On Earth Do Dwell

From Psalm 100

WILLIAM KETHE, 1561

LOUIS BOURGEOIS, (*cir.* 1510–1561)

1. All peo-ple that on earth do dwell, Sing to the Lord with cheer-ful voice, Him serve with praise, His praise forth
2. Know that the Lord is God in - deed, With - out our aid He did us make, We are His folk, He doth us

tell,   Come   ye   be - fore Him   and   re - joice.
feed,   And   for   His sheep He doth   us   take.

3.   O enter then His gates with praise,
     Approach with joy His courts unto;
     Praise, laud, and bless His name always,
     For it is seemly so to do.

4.   For why? The Lord our God is good,
     His mercy is forever sure;
     His truth at all times firmly stood,
     And shall from age to age endure.

O Sons And Daughters

JEAN TISSERAND, 1494
TR. JOHN M. NEALE (1818–1866)

FRENCH MELODY 15TH CENTURY

Al - le - lu - ia!___ Al - le - lu - ia!

Al - - - le - lu - - ia!

O   sons   and   daugh - ters, let___   us   sing!   The   King   of
That Eas - ter   morn,   at   break___   of   day,   The   faith - ful

Heaven, the glo - rious King, O'er death to - day___ rose___
wo - men went___ their way To seek the tomb___ where___

tri - umph - ing.___)
Je - sus lay.___ } Al - - - le - lu - - ia!

D.S.

D.S.

3. An angel clad in white they see,
   Who sat and spake unto the three,
   "Your Lord doth go to Galilee." Alleluia!

4. On this most holy day of days,
   To God your hearts and voices raise
   In laud and jubilee and praise. Alleluia!

Doxology

THOMAS KEN (1637–1711)

FROM THE *Genevan Psalter*, 1551

Praise God, from whom all bless-ings flow; Praise Him, all crea-tures here be-low;

Praise Him a-bove, ye heav'n-ly host; Praise Fa-ther, Son, and_ Ho-ly Ghost.

O What Their Joy And Their Glory Must Be

ATTRIB. TO PETER ABELARD (1079–1142)
TR. JOHN M. NEALE (1818–1866)

FRANÇOIS DE LA FEILLEE, 1805
HARM. BY JOHN B. DYKES, 1868

1. O what their joy and their glo - ry must be,
2. What are the Mon - arch, His court and His throne?

Those end - less Sab - baths the bless - ed ones see!
What are the peace and the joy that they own?

Crown for the val - iant, to wea - ry ones rest.
O that the blest ones who in it have share,

God shall be all___ and in all ev - er blest.___

All that they feel___ could as ful - ly de - clare!___

3. There, where no troubles distraction can bring,
   We the sweet anthems of Zion shall sing;
   While for Thy grace, Lord, their voices of praise
   Thy blessed people eternally raise.

4. There dawns no Sabbath, no Sabbath is o'er,
   Those Sabbath-keepers have one evermore;
   One and unending is that triumph song
   Which to the angels and us shall belong.

O Gladsome Light

GREEK 3RD CENTURY
TR. ROBERT BRIDGES (1844–1930)

ATTRIB. TO LOUIS BOURGEOIS (1510–1561)

1. O glad-some light,__ O__ grace of God the Fa-ther's face, Th'e-
2. Now, ere day fad-eth__ quite, We see the eve-ning light, Our
3. To Thee of right__ be-longs all praise of Ho-ly songs, O

ter-nal splen-dor wear-ing; Ce-les-tial, ho-ly blest, Our
wont-ed hymn out-pour-ing; Fa-ther of might un-known, Thee
Son of God, life-giv-er; Thee, there-fore, O most high, The

Sav-iour Je-sus Christ, Joy-ful in Thine ap-pear-ing.
His in-car-nate Son, And Ho-ly Spirit a-dor-ing.
world doth glo-ri-fy, And shall ex-alt for-ev-er.

213

Turn Back, O Man

OLD 124TH

LOUIS BOURGEOIS (1510–1561)

1. Turn back, O man, for - swear thy fool - ish ways.
2. Earth might be fair, and all men glad and wise,
3. Earth shall be fair, and all her peo - ple one:

Old now is earth, and none may count her days,
Age aft - er age their trag - ic em - pires rise,
Nor till that hour, shall God's whole will be done.

Yet Thou, her child, whose head is crowned with flame,
Built while they dream, and in that dream - ing weep:
Now, e - ven now, once more from earth to sky,

Still___ wilt not hear Thine in - ner God pro - claim,
Would___ man but wake from out his haunt - ed___ sleep,
Peals___ forth in joy man's old, un - daunt - ed___ cry,

Turn back, O man, for - swear Thy fool - ish___ ways.
Earth might be fair, and all men glad and___ wise.
"Earth shall be fair, and all her folk be___ one."

Praise Ye The Lord Of Hosts

CAMILLE SAINT SAËNS (1835–1921)

Praise ye the Lord of Hosts, Come and a - dore Him,

Bless His name and wor - ship Him in His ho - ly shrine

Sing, O ye Heav - ens, on earth be ye joy - ful,

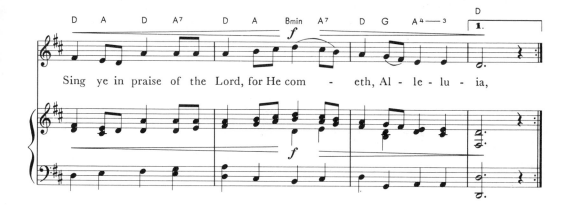

Sing ye in praise of the Lord, for He com - eth, Al - le - lu - ia,

ia, Al - le - lu - ia, Al - le - lu - ia, Al - le - lu -

ia,_____ Al - le - lu - ia, Al - le - lu - ia,_____

Al - le - lu – ia, Al - le - lu – ia, Sing, O ye

heav - ens, on earth be ye joy - ful Sing ye in praise of the

Lord, For he com — — eth, Al - le - lu – ia.

The Palms

JEAN BAPTISTE FAURE (1830–1914)

Moderato maestoso

O'er all the way, green palms and blos - soms gay,———

Are strewn this day in fes - tal prep - a - ra - tion, Where Je - sus comes to wipe our

tears a - way,——— E'en now the throng to wel - come Him pre-pare;

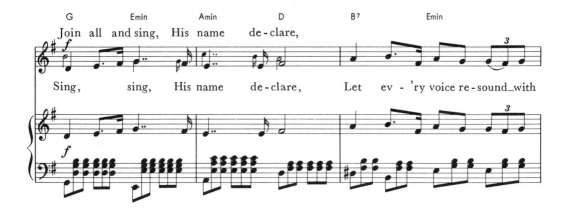

Join all and sing, His name de-clare,

Sing, sing, His name de-clare, Let ev-'ry voice re-sound with

Ho-san - na! praise be the Lord,

ac - cla-ma-tion, Join all and sing, His name de-clare

Bless Him who cometh to bring us sal-va - - - tion!

Christ, We Do All Adore Thee

From "The Seven Last Words of Christ"

THEODORE DUBOIS (1837–1924)

Christ, we do all a - dore — Thee, bless Thee, and praise Thee for - ev - er.

Christ, we do all a - dore Thee, bless Thee, and praise Thee for - ev - er.

Since by the ho - ly cross Thou hast the world from sin re - deem - ed.

Christ, we do all a - dore____ Thee, bless Thee, and praise Thee for - ev - er.

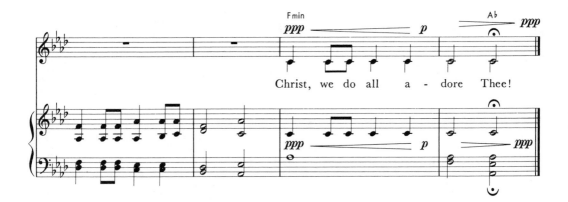

Christ, we do all a - dore Thee!

O Lord Most Holy

(Panis Angelicus)

CËSAR FRANCK (1822–1890)

Andante molto moderato

O Lord most ho - ly, O Lord most ho - ly,

O lov - ing Fa - ther, Thee would we be prais - ing,

Help us to know Thee, Praise Thee and love Thee,

Fa - ther, Fa - ther, Grant us Thy lov - ing care;

Fa - ther, Fa - ther, Guide and de - fend____ us.

Rule Thou our will-ful hearts, Keep Thee our wan-d'ring thought,

O lov-ing Fa - ther, let us find our rest in Thee:

When in temp - ta-tion's hour come with Thy might-y pow'r,

Thine aid,_O_ send_____ us. Hear_____ us in mer - cy.

Grant_____ us Thy mer - cy, So_____ shall we love and sing praise____ to

Thee.

Gentle Jesus

GABRIEL FAURE (1845–1924)

Scandinavian

Be Still, My Soul

KATHERINA VON SCHLEGEL (1697–?)
TR. JANE L. BORTHWICK (1813–1897)

JAN SIBELIUS (1865–1957)

1. Be still, my soul, the Lord is on thy side;
2. Be still, my soul, thy Lord doth un - der - take
3. Be still, my soul, the hour is has - t'ning on

Bear pa - tient - ly the cross of grief or pain,
To guide the fu - ture as He has the past.
When we shall be for - ev - er with the Lord,

Leave to thy God to or - der and pro - vide;
Thy hope, thy con - fi - dence let noth - ing shake;
When dis - ap - point - ment, grief, and fear are gone,

In ev - 'ry change He faith - ful will re - main
All now mys - te - rious shall be bright at last.
Sor - row for - got, love's pur - est joys re - stored,

Be still, my soul; thy best, thy heav'n - ly friend,
Be still, my soul; the waves and winds still know,
Be still, my soul; when change and tears are past,

Thro' thorn - y ways leads to a joy - ful end.
His voice who ruled them while He dwelt be - low.
All safe and bless - ed we shall meet at last.

Near Eastern

God The Omnipotent!

HENRY F. CHORLEY (1808–1872)
JOHN ELLERTON (1826–1893)

ALEXIS F. LVOV (1799–1870)

1. God the Om - ni - po-tent! King, who or - dain - est,
2. God the All mer - ci - ful! Earth hath for - sak - en
3. So shall Thy peo - ple, with thank - ful de - vo - tion,

Thun - der Thy clar - ion, the light - ning Thy sword;
Meek - ness and mer - cy, and slight - ed Thy word;
Praise Him who saved them from per - il and sword;

Show forth Thy pit - y on high____ where Thou reign - est:
Let not Thy wrath in its ter - rors a - wak - en;
Sing - ing in cho - rus from o - cean to o - cean,

Give to us peace___ in our time, O___ Lord.
Give to us peace___ in our time, O___ Lord.
Peace to the na - tions, and praise to the Lord.

Now On Land And Sea Descending

SAMUEL LONGFELLOW (1819–1892)   DIMITRI S. BORTNIANSKY (1752–1825)

1. Now on land and sea de-scend-ing, Brings the night its peace pro-found,
2. As the dark-ness deep-ens o'er us Lo! e-ter-nal stars a-rise:

Let our ves-per hymn be blend-ing With the Ho-ly calm a-round.
Hope and faith and love rise glo-rious, Shin-ing in the spir-it's skies.

Ju-bi-la-te! Ju-bi-la-te! Ju-bi-la-te!__ A-men!

Let our ves - per hymn be blend-ing With the Ho - ly___ calm a - round.
Hope and faith and love rise glo - rious, Shin - ing in the___ spir - it's skies.

Praise To The Living God

NEWTON MANN

"YIGDAL"

1. Praise to the liv - ing God! All prais-ed be His name,
2. Form - less, all love - ly forms, De - clare His lov - li - ness;
3. E - ter - nal life hath He Im - plant-ed in the soul;

Who was, and is, and is to be, For aye the same!
Ho - ly, no ho - li - ness of earth Can His ex - press.
His love shall be our strength and stay, While a - ges roll.

The One e - ter - nal God! Ere aught that now ap - pears:
Lo, He is Lord of all! Cre - a - tion speaks His praise,
Praise to the liv - ing God! All prais - ed be His Name,

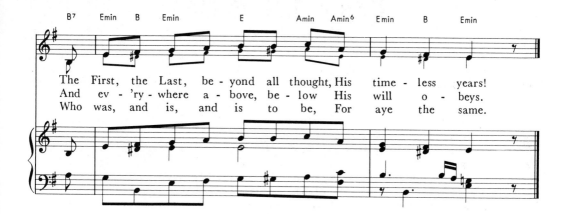

The First, the Last, be - yond all thought, His time - less years!
And ev - 'ry - where a - bove, be - low His will o - beys.
Who was, and is, and is to be, For aye the same.

Rock Of Ages

M. JASTROW (1829–1903)

SYNAGOGUE MELODY "MOOZ TSUR"

1. Rock of a - ges, let our song Praise Thy sav - ing pow - er;
2. Kind-ling new the ho - ly lamps, Priests ap - proved in suf - f'ring,
3. Chil - dren of the mar - tyr race, Wheth - er free or fet - tered,

Thou a - midst the rag - ing foes, Wast our shelt -'ring tow - er.
Pu - ri - fied the na - tion's shrine, Brought to God their of - f'ring.
Wake the ech - oes of the songs Where ye may be scat - tered.

Fur - ious, they as - sailed us, But Thine arm a - vailed___ us,
And His courts sur - round - ing Hear, in joy a - bound - ing,
Yours the mes - sage cheer - ing, That the time is near - ing

And   Thy word,   Broke their sword   When our own strength failed____ us.
Hap - py throngs,   Sing - ing songs   With   a   might - y   sound - ing.
Which will see   All   men free,   Ty - rants dis - ap - pear - ing.

Some Notes about the Hymns

America the Beautiful

Kathryn Lee Bates, with a group of teachers from Wellesley College took a trip west in 1893. First they visited the exposition in Chicago. Then, going on to Colorado, they gazed in wonder at the mountains and plains from the top of Pikes Peak. Miss Bates, inspired by the beauty of the scenery, wrote the four-stanza poem which was printed two years later in a church magazine. Although set to music many times, the tune used for "America the Beautiful" today is "Materna" composed by Samuel Ward. Many Americans consider this to be the nation's most appealing patriotic hymn.

God of Our Fathers
Whose Almighty Hand

The words of this hymn were written in the tiny village of Brandon, Vermont in 1876. The occasion was the town's celebration of the one hundredth anniversary of the Declaration of Independence. The writer, Daniel Crane Roberts, born in Long Island, New York, was minister in Brandon, and this hymn is his major claim to fame. At first it was sung to the "Russian Hymn," the national anthem of Russia, composed by Alexis Lvov. The tune used now was composed by William Warren, an organist at Saint Thomas Church in New York City. The dramatic trumpet calls at the beginning of each stanza make this hymn effective as a processional and serviceable for patriotic occasions.

Battle Hymn of the Republic

During the Civil War, Julia Ward Howe visited a Union Army outpost near Washington, D.C. A surprise Confederate attack forced Mrs. Howe and her companion, Reverend James Clarke, to return to Washington. On the way back they heard the Union troops singing a rousing camp meeting hymn to which words commemorating John Brown's martyrdom at Harper's Ferry had been set. Reverend Clarke suggested that someone should write different words for this fine tune. That night Mrs. Howe wrote this famous poem. It was first published in the *Atlantic Monthly*. The hymn became the marching song of the North, even though the tune had been composed by a southerner, William Steffe.

This Is My Father's World

Maltbie Babcock was a Presbyterian minister who, as a student at Syracuse University, was an outstanding athlete, a leader of the glee club, orchestra, and dramatic club. He loved nature, and when he was a pastor in Lockport, New York, he would walk up a hill in the northern end of town to see the view of Lake Ontario and to communicate with God. This poem, expressive of his feelings, is filled with the splendor of life. The hymn tune also expresses a nature theme. "Terra Beata" means "Blessed Earth." Franklin Sheppard, a friend of Babcock and an officer in his church, composed the tune.

Ancient of Days

This hymn was written by Bishop William C. Doane in 1886 to celebrate the two hundredth anniversary of Albany, New York, the first chartered city in America. A dignified hymn full of Old Testament references, it is often sung as a hymn to the Trinity at Thanksgiving, or as a processional for large festivals. The tune was composed by John Albert Jeffery, an Englishman who came to America in 1876 to act as organist and choirmaster of the cathedral in Albany.

Dear Lord and Father of Mankind

John Greenleaf Whittier is one of America's best known poets. His life and poetry were closely connected with the Quaker faith, and he was known as "The Quaker Poet." The idea for this hymn was taken from a seventeen-stanza poem, "The Brewing of Soma," a poem describing the Hindu custom of preparing and drinking an intoxicating brew, soma (a mixture of honey and milk), which produced a frenzy of activity. This was supposed to be a way of communicating with their God. Whittier's hymn contrasts this frenetic activity with the quiet spiritual ways of Christians. Some of the words recall pictures from the Bible. In verse one, "reclothe us" is taken from the story of Jesus casting out a legion of devils from a man, after which the man was found clothed and in his right mind. Although Whittier was not a prolific hymn writer, his religious poetry is so universal that all hymnals could contain his works. The tune for this hymn was composed by Frederick C. Maker for the *Congregational Hymnary* in 1887.

Rock of Ages

This hymn has given many people comfort in times of fear and death, and has proven to be one of the most popular hymns in the English language. The writer, Augustus Toplady, was an ardent Calvinist, and the hymn was the result of a lengthy and heated argument with John Wesley fought through sermons, letters, and magazines. It was published in the *Gospel Magazine* as the climax to an article in which Toplady compared England's inability to pay her national debt with man's inability to live without sinning —a slap at Wesley's claim that a believer could live without sinning. The tune was composed by one of the great leaders in American church music in the nineteenth century, Thomas Hastings, who composed over one thousand tunes using many *noms de plume*. An excellent choral conductor, Hastings reputedly could read a score upside down.

Oh My Father

Eliza Roxey Snow, the author of this hymn, was a remarkable Mormon woman. Born in Becket, Massachusetts in 1804, she was brought up as a Baptist. Her poetic talents were discovered early when at twenty-two she wrote a requiem for John Adams and Thomas Jefferson, both of whom died on July 4, 1826. After being converted to the Church of the Latter-Day Saints, she served for a while as governess in the home of Joseph Smith, the prophet. Influenced greatly by him, she devoted her whole life to the gospel. In 1842 they were married. "Oh My Father," written in 1843, was undoubtedly inspired by their discussions on resurrection and the relationship of God and man. Although set to many tunes by Later-Day Saint composers, "My Redeemer" by James Mc Granahan is the favorite one. It was sung at the dedication of the Tabernacle in Salt Lake and at the 1893 Chicago World's Fair. One year after the hymn was written, Joseph Smith was martyred. Eliza Smith continued writing songs. Later, she went to Salt Lake where she married Brigham Young.

Nearer, My God, to Thee

Known as the favorite hymn of President McKinley, and sung by hundreds when the Titanic sank in 1912, this hymn was written by an English woman, Sarah Adams, in response to her minister's request for hymns for his new hymnbook. The words are based on Jacob's experience at Bethel when he learned that God would always be with him. The hymn was first sung in 1840 and was included in the 1841 edition of Reverend Fox's *Hymns and Anthems*. Sarah and her sister Elizabeth contributed a major portion of the material for this collection. The hymn gained great popularity when Lowell Mason composed the tune "Bethany" for it. In the Boston Peace Jubilee of 1872, this hymn was sung by nearly fifty thousand voices.

Rejoice, Ye Pure in Heart

Edwards H. Plumtre was the Dean of the Wells Cathedral. He wrote this hymn as a processional to be used in a choir festival in Peterborough Cathedral. Joy is the key emotion expressed by the words which may have been inspired by Philippeans 4:4—"Rejoice in the Lord alway; and again I say rejoice." Although the ten verses originally written for the hymn are too numerous for American churches, this would not be the case for a choir festival in an English cathedral where the processional alone might take thirty minutes. Arthur Messiter, the composer of the tune, "Marion," named after his mother, played the organ at the Trinity Episcopal Church in New York City for thirty-one years.

Gently Raise the Sacred Strain

The Mormon poet, William Phelps, wrote the words to this hymn without realizing that after being set to music by Thomas Griggs, it would be used as the theme song for the Tabernacle Choir's daily radio broadcast. The poem is an expression of gratitude for the Sabbath Day and a commentary on its meaning. The composer, Griggs, an Englishman, immigrated to Boston with his mother in 1857. After the Civil War he went to Utah. There he played in bands and became a choir leader. He sang in the Tabernacle Choir, and was appointed its director while on a mission in England.

As the Dew from Heaven Distilling

The circumstances surrounding the writing of this hymn are unknown. The Mormon, Parley Pratt, intended it as an invocation to the Lord to open heaven's windows and let the truth fall as dew upon the congregation. The composer, Joseph Daynes, has twenty-seven compositions included in the Latter-Day Saints' hymnal. At the age of sixteen, Daynes was appointed organist at the old Tabernacle. When the new Mormon Tabernacle in Salt Lake City was completed, he continued as organist there. He instituted the first recitals on the great organ in Salt Lake City. The noon organ recitals are still a tradition today.

Sweet Hour of Prayer

This gospel song describing the welcome comfort of prayer was written by William Walford. Walford, who made his living by carving items from ivory and preaching at various churches for his minister friends, was blind. He dedicated the poem to a Congregational minister, Thomas Salmon, who in turn gave it to the *New York Observer*. Fourteen years later a New York organist and composer, William Bradbury, set it to music.

Amazing Grace

After a tempestuous and, by his own account, wicked early life, John Newton was converted and became a leader in the Evangelical movement in England. When he obtained an assignment to minister at Olney, he wrote a book of hymns for his parishioners' use. His friend William Cowper helped him in this task. "Amazing Grace" appears as number 41 in the Olney collection. The tune used in this book is from William Walker's *Southern Harmony*, one of the most popular shaped note hymnals used in southern rural areas in the nineteenth century.

Blessed Assurance

Phoebe Knapp, a composer, was the daughter of an evangelist and wife of the founder of the Metropolitan Life Insurance Company. In 1873 Mrs. Knapp visited Fanny Crosby, the famous blind gospel hymn writer, and asked her to write words for a piece of music. The result was "Blessed Assurance." Later the two collaborated on "Open the Gates of the Temple," a favorite Palm Sunday or Easter solo, which has since been arranged as a choral anthem as well. Miss Crosby who lived to be eighty-four, wrote more than 8,000 songs and used 216 pen names.

Love Divine, All Loves Excelling

Originally called "Hymn for Those that Sin and Those that Have Redemption in the Blood of Christ," this speaks of the Deity as a God of love. The fact that very few early hymns did this may account for its popularity. There are many scriptural references in this hymn, as well as in others by Charles Wesley. This tune was composed by John Zundel, a native of Germany who became organist at the Plymouth Church in Brooklyn, New York. He helped improve congregational singing in his church, and composed tunes for the *Plymouth Collection*.

My Faith Looks Up to Thee

After graduating from Yale, Ray Palmer taught in a girls' school to support himself while he studied theol-

ogy. He wrote this hymn at the age of twenty-one. It was a spontaneous expression of what Christ meant to him. Palmer put it into his notebook, not intending that anyone else should read it. Two years later in Boston he met Lowell Mason, one of America's first great hymn composers and the founder of public school music. Mason told him he was looking for new hymns to be included in a hymnbook to be published soon. Palmer referred to his notebook where he found "My Faith Looks Up to Thee." Mason made a copy of the hymn in a nearby store, and told Palmer that he would be known to posterity for the words. Mason composed the tune, "Oliver," for the hymn.

I Love to Tell the Story

Arabella Katherine Hankey was a Sunday school teacher in a London suburb. She started a Bible class for girls in London when she was eighteen. As a result of a trip to South Africa, she became interested in missions, to which cause she gave all the royalties from her gospel songs. This hymn is extracted from the second section of a long poem entitled "The Old, Old Story." The tune was composed by William Gustavius Fischer, a piano dealer who composed a number of melodies for gospel songs. This hymn probably appeared first in a Sunday school leaflet issued by the firm of Gould and Fischer. Leaflets of gospel songs used to be issued by business firms as a means of advertising.

Into the Woods My Master Went

Sidney Lanier was a Georgian who at first wrote hymns for his own enjoyment, not realizing that other people would find pleasure in his writings. He contributed fourteen volumes of prose and ten books of poetry to the field of hymnody. This hymn was written at the age of thirty-nine when he was dying of tuberculosis and sought solace in the woods. The tune was composed by Peter Lutkin, former Dean of the Northwestern School of Music and prominent midwestern church musician.

What a Friend We Have in Jesus

Joseph Scriven, a graduate of Trinity College in Dublin, wrote the words of this hymn. Ira D. Sankey, the famous gospel hymn singer, has given an account of how this hymn was written in his book, *My Life and Sacred Songs:* apparently a neighbor of Scriven discovered the manuscript while sitting up with him during an illness. When questioned about it, Scriven replied that he had written the hymn to comfort his mother, and that he had not intended anyone else to see it. Sankey included it in one of his gospel hymnals, and it is still a favorite gospel hymn, today. Charles Converse, an American scholar and musician, composed the tune.

All Hail the Power of Jesus' Name

This regal hymn appears in many hymnals in three musical settings. It was first sung to a tune called "Miles Lane" composed by a London organist, William Shrubsole. A Massachusetts carpenter, Oliver Holden, composed the florid "Coronation" tune that is popular with many church choirs. A third version, "Diadem," was composed by an English hatter, James Ellor, for his Sunday school's anniversary celebration. The words are by Edward Perronet who, for a time, was a follower of the Wesleys.

How Firm a Foundation

This was a favorite hymn of Presidents Andrew Jackson and Theodore Roosevelt, and of General Robert E. Lee, who requested that it be sung at his funeral. The name of the poet is uncertain. The hymn is listed under "K" in a book called *Selections of*

Hymns from the Best Authors compiled by Dr. John Rippon in 1787. Suggestions for whom the anonymous Mr. K. might have been are: George Keith, who was Dr. Rippon's son-in-law; or Robert Keene, the precentor of Reverend Rippon's Baptist Church in London. The latter is more probable since he was a musician. "Adeste Fidelis," the tune to which this is most commonly sung, was composed by J. F. Wade, an Englishman who taught in France, but there are also American folk-like settings.

I Would Be True

Harold Arnold Walter, who taught English in Japan when he was a young man, sent home to his mother this poem which expresses his personal religious credo. She sent it to *Harper's Bazaar* in 1907. Later Joseph Peek, a friend of Walter's, composed the tune for it. Peek, just an amateur musician, had an organist and composer friend notate and harmonize the tune. This hymn, a favorite with youth, is also appropriate for New Year or dedication services.

Blest Be the Tie that Binds

The Reverend John Fawcett had decided to move to a large Baptist parish in London, which was professionally more challenging and also paid a higher salary than his small parish in Wainsgate could afford. His unhappy congregation helped him prepare to move. Just as the Fawcetts were ready to go, the Reverend, impressed by the devoted love of his parishioners, decided to stay. He wrote this hymn for his congregation. Over the years his work prospered. He opened a school which trained preachers, published a hymnal, and built a new church. Later, when offered anything he wanted by King George III, Fawcett replied that the king could offer him nothing better than the love of his own people. This favorite hymn, with music by Lowell

Mason, the respected American hymn composer and educator, is often sung at the close of a service.

O Brother Man

Whittier wrote this hymn during the Mexican War and it is consistent with his anti-slavery convictions. The text is from his poem, "Worship," written in 1848. Joseph W. Lerman composed the tune.

Rise Up, O Men of God

William Pearson Merrill wrote this hymn in answer to a request by the editor of a magazine called *The Continent*. The words came to him after reading an article, "The Church of Strong Men," while on a Lake Michigan steamer. This is sometimes called the hymn of exclamation points, as there is one in each stanza. The hymn has had many musical settings, the two best known being that of William Henry Walter, a New York organist, and the setting in this volume composed by Aaron Williams.

Where Cross the Crowded Ways of Life

Caleb Winchester, a member of the editorial committee that was revising the Methodist hymnal, asked Reverend Frank Mason North to write a hymn on a missionary theme. For inspiration North drew from his experience in the slum section of New York City.

Come, Come, Ye Saints

This is the best known Mormon hymn. The poem was written by William Clayton to fit a Georgian tune found in *The Sacred Harp*, a collection by J. T. White. This collection, like Walker's *Southern Harmony*, was a favorite shaped-note hymnal in the rural southwest. Copies are still extant today. Clayton was among the first group of Mormons to migrate westward from New York to Utah. His wife remained in Illinois in order to give birth to their son. Her letter following the birth closed with "all is well." Clayton wrote his stanzas of comfort and strength, retaining the significant line, "all is well."

Simple Gifts

This hymn is sung everywhere in the congregations of the United Society of Believers. Shaker is the name given to this society which began in England in 1706. Shakers first came to America in 1774 and organized a society at Watervliet, New York. This was the first communal organization in the United Society. Members of this society are called Shakers because during religious exercises their intense emotions cause them to quiver and shake. This hymn extols simplicity, the most pervasive of Shaker virtues. Both speech and dress were plain, and thoughts and policies were direct and honest. This is a lively piece, being marked *allegro* in the original manuscript. Aaron Copland, the renowned twentieth century composer, included this tune in his ballet, *Appalachian Spring*.

My Shepherd Will Supply My Need

This hymn is called a white spiritual. These songs were sung by people who lived in the rural south in the nineteenth century. The white spiritual influenced both the Negro spiritual and the white gospel song as religious song forms. This hymn, as found in southern hymnals, was printed in shaped note form.

Jesus Walked This Lonesome Valley

This is a beautiful spiritual which likens the life and trials of Jesus to that of man. Because of their popularity, spirituals are often heard at concerts either as solos, choral arrangements, or instrumental transcriptions. This is a favorite with choirs, the first half often being sung in canonic form.

There Is a Balm in Gilead

This sustained, lyrical spiritual is an expression of the slaves' anticipation of a better life after death.

Ev'ry Time I Feel the Spirit

One of the most beautiful forms of American sacred music is the spiritual, at once expressing the solace of religion and hope for eventual happiness, and freedom from misery. The extraordinary variety of rhythmic patterns found in spirituals is derived from the Negroes' African heritage. Almost every phrase of this spiritual uses an offbeat or syncopated rhythm which lends a feeling of joy and vitality to the song.

Let Us Break Bread Together

There are two types of spirituals. One type, fast and lively is often referred to as a "shout." The second type, here, is slow and sustained. In some churches this spiritual is used as a Communion hymn.

Swing Low, Sweet Chariot

One of the most popular of the Negro spirituals, this tune utilizes the call and response technique in which a soloist sings a line and the congregation answers.

Were You There?

This spiritual is a poignant evocation of the crucifixion. It was first published in William E. Barton's *Old Plantation Hymns* in Boston in 1899. Since spirituals, like many folk songs, were spontaneously composed and spread by word of mouth, changes in both words and melody are common. The present version appeared in *Folk Songs of the American Negro* by John and Frederick Work, published in 1907.

He's Got the Whole World in His Hands

This spiritual is a favorite of the famed contralto, Marian Anderson, who during her illustrious career, performed it all over the world. It expresses belief in a divine power who holds every man's destiny in his hands.

The Rosary

The words to this song were written by Robert Cameron Rogers and printed in a magazine in 1894. Ethelbert Nevin, who saw the poem as a clipping sent to him by his mother, liked it, and in a single setting sketched the music. The song was received coldly at its first performance on February 15, 1898 in New York City, but in a Boston recital two days later it was a big success. Its popularity has continued ever since.

Recessional

Reginald de Koven, the son of a clergyman, was born in Middletown, Connecticut, and was educated at Oxford and on the Continent. Returning to the United States, he became one of the foremost American composers of light opera, and was also a music critic and conductor of the Philharmonic Orchestra in Washington. His best known work was *Robin Hood*, in which the song, "Oh, Promise Me," occurs.

The Holy City

Stephen Adams was the pseudonym of an English composer and baritone, Michael Maybrick. Many songs that Maybrick sang attained great popularity in his day. He composed "The Holy City" originally as a concert song. The words are by F. E. Weatherly.

My Task

The composer, Mrs. Emma L. Ashford, as a young girl, sang in the village church choir, and by the age of twelve was a chuch organist in southern Illinois. In her adult years, she taught piano, organ, and harmony, played for church services and served as editor of a monthly publication, *The Organist*. She wrote over three hundred anthems, several cantatas, sacred solos and duets, song cycles, organ works, and piano pieces. "My Task" is probably the best known of her compositions.

The Lord Bless You and Keep You

This well-known benediction is based on the book of Numbers in the Old Testament and is sometimes called the "Aaronic blessing" because Aaron, the high priest of the Israelites, pronounced these words on the children of Israel following their departure from Egypt. The musical setting was composed by the American organist and teacher, Peter Lutkin, who was one of the founders of the Northwestern University School of Music, Evanston, Illinois, where from 1895 until his death in 1931 he was dean.

Holy, Holy, Holy

Written by Reginald Heber for Trinity Sunday which occurs eight weeks after Easter, this hymn of great dignity and power seeks to define the natures of the Triune God (three in one: Father, Son, Holy Spirit). John Dykes composed the tune, "Nicaea," named after the Council of Nicaea where the Doctrine of the Trinity was proclaimed.

Praise, My Soul, the King of Heaven

The Anglican minister, Henry Francis Lyte, wrote hymns for his parish, a little fishing village, Lower Brixham. This particular hymn is exultant and jubilant in mood, whereas his earlier hymns were introspective due to his poor health. The melody, "Regent Square," by Henry Smart, editor of

two tune books, is an excellent example of English hymn tune. It is said that he did for the English hymn tune what Bach did for the chorale.

O God, Our Help in Ages Past

Isaac Watts is one of the great names in English hymnody. While still a young man he spoke out against poor congregational singing which he attributed to the metrical psalms. Possessing unusual skills in rhyming, he proceeded to rectify the situation. Two kinds of hymns contributed to Watts' fame as a religious poet. In the first group were Watts' completely original compositions, called the hymns of human composure. The second category consisted of psalm adaptations couched in modern Christian language. Watts composed nearly all the hymns for his volume, *Hymns and Spiritual Songs*. "O God Our Help in Ages Past," written in 1714 and based on Psalm 90, is one of the greatest in English hymnody. The tune is attributed to Dr. William Croft, who is said to have influenced George F. Handel.

Faith of Our Fathers

Frederick Faber was an Anglican priest who was converted to Catholicism as a result of his association with John Henry Newman. Faber wrote some hymns when he noted that English Catholics did not have a wealth of hymns comparable to the Protestants. At the time of his death he had written three volumes containing a total of 150 hymns. Since he wrote all of his hymns after becoming a Catholic, some have to be edited for use in Protestant churches. For instance, the first verse of this hymn is omitted from Protestant hymnals because it expresses hope that England would return to the Roman Church. ("Faith of our fathers, Mary's prayers shall win our country back to thee.") The last stanza is a beautiful expression of our supreme test of all Christians—the ability to love both friend and enemy. The tune was composed by Henri Frederick Hemy, an English professor of music, organist, and piano teacher.

Eternal Father Strong to Save

This hymn, also known as the "Navy Hymn," was written by William Whiting who was master of the Winchester College Choristers School in England. It is the only hymn for which he is known, and it is the most widely used hymn of the sea. The verses are based on the Trinity formula; stanza one being addressed to the Father, stanza two to the Son, and three to the Spirit. Stanza four unites all of them. The melody, "Melita," (an ancient name for Malta, the island on which Saint Paul was shipwrecked) was composed by John Dykes. Dr. Dykes was a prominent English hymn composer in the latter nineteenth century. His musical talents were discovered as a boy, and later he studied music at Cambridge. Finally he took Holy Orders and served as precentor at Durham Cathedral, where he composed most of his hymn tunes.

All Things Bright and Beautiful

Mrs. Cecil F. Alexander wrote many hymns for her Sunday school class, as she thought it a good idea to learn about Christianity through poetry. Her *Verses for Holy Seasons* contained a hymn for every Sunday and all the other holidays celebrated in the Anglican Church. Another volume was entitled *Hymns for Little Children*. The tune for this hymn is an arrangement by William H. Hewlett of a traditional English melody. Hewlett was an organist in various churches in Canada and the head of the Hamilton Conservatory of Music, Hamilton, Ontario.

God that Madest Earth and Heaven

Reginald Heber, the first missionary bishop of Calcutta, India, wrote only one stanza of this hymn, an evening prayer. Archbishop Whatley added a second stanza at a later date. The tune is an old Welsh melody popularly known as "All Through the Night."

Immortal, Invisible

This hymn of praise to God was first printed in *Hymns of Christ and Christian Life* by the Reverend Walter Chalmers Smith. It is an apostrophe of nature to God based on Timothy I: "Now unto the King eternal, immortal, invisible, the only wise God be honor and glory forever and ever Amen." The mountains, clouds, and vegetation are suggestive of God's constant justice, his continual love, and the renewal of the tides of life through the seasons. Smith filled several volumes with his poetry. The tune is a Welsh folk song, "Joanna," known in England as "St. Denis."

God of Grace and God of Glory

This hymn was written by the famous Baptist clergyman, Harry Emerson Fosdick, for use as a processional at the dedication of the Riverside Church in New York City in 1930. Fosdick, who received many honorary degrees, was prominent as an author and educator, and was one of America's outstanding preachers. This hymn is most often sung to the Welsh tune, "Cum Rhondda."

The King of Love My Shepherd Is

This is a well-known version of the twenty-third psalm. Henry Baker, clergyman of the Church of England and vicar of Monkland, wrote it for the appendix of *Hymns Ancient and Modern*, to which he also contributed Latin translations and hymn tunes. Baker is said to have uttered words from the third stanza of this hymn before he died. In his lifetime he composed thirty-three hymns as well as editing hymnals and devotional books.

His hymns are simple and many of them are tenderly sad. John Dykes wrote the melody.

O Zion, Haste

Mrs. Mary A. Thomson contributed more than forty hymns to *The Churchman* and *The Living Church*. This missionary hymn was inspired one night while Mrs. Thomson was attending her daughter who was sick with typhoid. Three years later she finished it. Then, a hymnal editor matched her words to a tune, "Tidings," by James Walch. Walch, an Englishman, was director of the Boston Philharmonic Society and an honorary organist at the parish church in Barrow-in-Furness.

Come, Thou Long Expected Jesus

Wesley wrote this as an Advent hymn. Advent is the season in the Christian calendar which includes the four Sundays before Christmas. Wesley included this in a collection entitled *Hymns For the Nativity of Our Lord*. The first tune used with it was an adaptation of "If With All Your Hearts," a tenor solo from Mendelssohn's oratorio, *Elijah*. Prichard's "Hyfrydol," the tune used in this book, has since become the preferred setting.

Christ the Lord Is Risen Today

There is probably no other hymn that is more frequently sung at Easter services than this hymn by Charles Wesley. The custom of greeting the rising sun with hallelujahs, begun in early Christian times, is reinforced in this celebration of the resurrection. Once he was converted there was scarcely a day that Wesley didn't work on a hymn. Between thirty and eighty years of age he wrote over 6,000 hymns. The tune appeared in a collection called *Lyra Davidica*, compiled by an unknown source in 1708. The only copy of this book is in the British Museum.

Come Ye Faithful, Raise the Strain

This is a hymn of hope and gladness written for the first Sunday after Easter by the great preacher, John of Damascus, who was later canonized as a saint. John lived to be 104 years old, spending much of his life in Mar Saba, a desolate monastery near the Red Sea. During this time, he achieved a reputation as a great hymn writer and music scholar, for not only did he write both words and music for a hymnbook used in the daily prayer services of the church, but he developed a system for music notation. The subjects of his hymns encompassed the whole life of Jesus. This particular one expresses faith in the resurrection. The music for this hymn was composed by Arthur S. Sullivan, known primarily for the operettas written with William Gilbert, but who was also a church organist and hymn composer.

The Church's One Foundation

Samuel Stone wrote this hymn for two reasons. First, he was attempting to interpret the Apostles' Creed for those who recited it without realizing the meaning of the words. The second purpose was to take sides in a religious dispute then raging between Bishop Gray and Bishop Colenso of South Africa. Colenso had attacked the first five books of the Bible as irrational and unscientific. Stone sided with Gray, who supported the traditionalist views of the Bible. This hymn has been translated into several languages and is often used as a processional or for dedication services. This and two similar pieces based on the Apostles' Creed were included by Stone in a small book called *Lyra Fidelium*. The tune was composed by Samuel Sebastian Wesley, a grandson of Charles Wesley.

When Morning Gilds the Skies

This is a translation of a German hymn whose source is unknown. From the *Katholisches Gesangbuch* with the title, "A Christian Greeting," the hymn became a favorite with the Saint Paul's congregation in London. The translator was Edward Caswall, who along with John Mason Neale restored a rich heritage of ancient hymns during the Oxford Revival Movement in England. Caswall, an Anglican, later left the Church of England to become a Catholic and spent his later life with John Henry Newman ministering to poor, sick children. The tune, "Laudes Domini," by Joseph Barnby is a good example of a type of English hymn popular at the beginning of this century.

Jesus, Lover of My Soul

This, one of Charles Wesley's earliest hymns, was originally published by the Wesley brothers in 1740 in their hymn-book, *Hymns and Sacred Poems*. It is now found in nearly all Protestant hymnals and has been translated for missionary use. Nobody knows how it was written, although several unauthenticated stories have been proposed. The tune was composed by Simeon Marsh, but for another hymn. Marsh, a Sunday school superintendent, organist, and choir leader in Sherburne, New York, composed this melody while on the way to one of his singing schools. He fitted his tune with the words for the hymn, "Mary At Her Saviour's Tomb." About one hundred years later Thomas Hastings, a great leader in nineteenth century American church music and a composer of 600 hymns, fitted Marsh's music to Wesley's hymn.

Onward Christian Soldiers

The Reverend Sabine Baring-Gould had arranged an outing for the children of Harbury Bridge, England, where he was curate in charge of mission work. Since the children were to hike from the church to the village, he asked his helpers to find a good marching tune. When they could offer

no suggestions, Baring-Gould composed one himself. The Reverend used a theme from the slow movement of Haydn's *Symphony in D* for the tune. However, today the hymn is sung to Sir Arthur Sullivan's "Saint Gertrude," composed in 1871.

Now the Day Is Over

The Reverend Sabine Baring-Gould was an extremely prolific literary figure during the Victorian era. The catalog of the British Museum shows more titles by him than any other writer of his time. He published eighty-five works in fifty-two years on subjects of religion, travel, mythology, history, and folklore. *Grove's Dictionary of Music and Musicians* credits him with being a pioneer in the collection of English folk songs, and with having influenced Cecil J. Sharp, a renowned English folklorist, to devote his life to this type of work. "Now the Day is Over" is an evening prayer based on Proverbs 3:24— "When thou liest down, thou shalt not be afraid: yea thou shalt lie down and thy sleep shall be sweet." It was written as a children's hymn for the youngsters of Harbury Bridge, England, while he was curate in charge of that district. Joseph Barnby, a prolific English hymn composer in the late nineteenth century, composed the tune. Barnby, also a distinguished choral conductor, was knighted in 1892.

All Praise to Thee My God This Night

This is another hymn by Thomas Ken, a great preacher and rigid moralist, who won favor with England's King Charles II. Probably it was Ken's courageous refusal to comply with royal commands that stirred the King's admiration. It is told that once when Charles ordered Ken to receive Nell Gwyn, the King's mistress, as guest, the churchman ordered his roof removed so that Nell Gwyn would not wish to remain. This evening hymn is from Ken's *Manual of Prayer,* written while he was chaplain at Winchester College. The tune is by Thomas Tallis, whose career as organist spanned the reigns of Henry VIII, Edward VII, and Elizabeth I.

Abide With Me

This is another hymn written by Henry Lyte for the village of Brixham. This well-known hymn which likens death to the stages of night, was written for Lyte's last Sunday at Brixham, before he died of tuberculosis. "Abide With Me" has always been sung to William Henry Monk's music which was inspired by a beautiful sunset and personal sorrow, and composed in ten minutes. Monk was the editor of the most famous collection of hymns to come out of nineteenth century England, *Hymns Ancient and Modern.*

Lead, Kindly Light

This prayerful hymn was composed by John Henry Newman, an Anglican clergyman who later became a cardinal in the Roman Catholic Church. It was written aboard a ship imperiled by fog in the Mediterranean Sea. This experience is probably the basis for the hymn's imagery, although it is known that during this same period Dr. Newman was undergoing a spiritual crisis in which he was "led on by God's hand blindly, not knowing whither he is taking me." The tune, written by John Dykes was said by Newman to be responsible for the hymn's great popularity.

O Perfect Love

This is probably the best known wedding hymn. It was written in fifteen minutes by Dorothy B. Gurney, and was first sung at her sister's wedding. The words speak of Christ as perfect love and perfect life, both of which have great significance for the rite of marriage. The tune, by Joseph Barnby,

the composer of "Now the Day is Over," has also been adapted as an anthem for chorus.

These Things Shall Be

In one of John Addington Symonds' volumes was a poem called "A Vista." This hymn is taken from that poem. The fear of a war in Europe lies at the bottom of this plea for a new race which would shun war. The hymn was widely used during World War I. The tune, "Truro," is taken from a collection of psalm and hymn tunes called *Psalmodia Evangelica,* probably compiled by Thomas Williams in 1789; however, some authorities have assigned this piece to Charles Burney.

Once to Every Man and Nation

An English hymnologist, Garret Horder, saw the possibilities for a hymn in James Russell Lowell's poem, "The Present Crisis," which had been written as a protest against the Mexican War. Horder picked sixteen lines from the poem and arranged them to form this passionate hymn. The melody, "Ton-Y-Botel" (Tune in Bottle) was composed as part of an anthem by the Welshman Thomas John Williams. The legend that the tune was found in a bottle was probably made up by a young man, who sang it at a social gathering before it was well-known. This hymn is especially effective when sung by a large group of men.

Jerusalem the Golden

In A.D. 910 the Abbey of Cluny was founded on the site of William Duke of Aquitaine's hunting lodge in France. It became the most important monastery in all of Europe. The abbots of Cluny were men of exceptional character, and western civilization is indebted to them and their monks for the spread of the Romanesque style of architecture. In about 1109 Bernard, born in Brittany, came to the abbey.

Since that time he has been known as Bernard of Cluny. While there he wrote a 3000-line poem, "De Contemptu Mundi" (In Contempt of the World). This hymn begins with a description of the peace and glory of heaven. Dr. John Mason Neale, an outstanding figure in the Oxford Movement in nineteenth century England, translated the hymn. Two other hymns have been adapted from his translation: "Brief Life Here Our Portion" and "For Thee, O Dear, Dear Country." The tune for "Jerusalem the Golden," composed by Alexander Ewing was originally meant for "For Thee, O Dear, Dear Country." Ewing, a lawyer, was held in high esteem in Scotland as an amateur musician.

For All the Saints

Bishop How, called "the poor man's bishop" because he was bishop of a slum section of East London, wrote this hymn for All Saints Day. It has since proved fitting for use on Memorial Day also. Bishop How wrote all of his sixty hymns between 1858-1871 while he was rector in a farming village on the Welsh border, and all of his hymns embody his ideals of simplicity and reverence. Another Englishman, Ralph Vaughan Williams, editor of *The English Hymnal*, composed the music. The composer began writing his own melodies when the editors of *Hymns Ancient and Modern* refused to grant him permission to use some of their tunes. Vaughan Williams, recognized as one of the most distinguished composers in English history, was also co-editor with Martin Shaw and Percy Dearmer of *Songs of Praise* and *The Oxford Book of Carols*.

Brother James' Air

James Leith Macbeth Bain was known by the name of Brother James. This lovely melody came to him spontaneously. The text, a paraphrase of the twenty-third psalm, has been set to music innumerable times by composers of all eras.

God So Loved the World

This piece is from an oratorio, *The Crucifixion*, by Sir John Stainer. It is his best known composition, beloved by American church choirs. Stainer was the son of a musical parish schoolmaster. He was a choir boy at Saint Paul's Cathedral, and later became an organist there. When in 1883 he had to give up his Saint Paul's position because of his failing vision, Queen Victoria knighted him.

He Shall Feed His Flock

This alto aria from the first part of Handel's oratorio, *Messiah*, tenderly expresses the text from Isaiah 40:11 which portrays Christ as the good shepherd. Handel composed *Messiah*, the eleventh of his twenty-three oratorios, in just three weeks.

Holy Art Thou, Lord God Almighty

Also known as "Largo" or "Ombra Mai Fu," this aria appears in the first scene of Handel's opera, *Xerxes*. After Handel finished this opera in 1738, the Haymarket Theatre in London only gave it five performances.

Thanks Be to Thee

This beautiful melody from one of Handel's cantatas with instruments is thought to have been interpolated into his oratorio, *Israel in Egypt*, as an added number.

A Mighty Fortress Is Our God

Martin Luther wrote both words and melody to this strong affirmation of faith. It was written in 1529 when the Lutheran movement was being severely persecuted. The hymn text, taken from Psalm 46: "God is our refuge and our strength," became the battle cry of the Lutheran Reformation. Luther's religious accomplishments were great. Not only did he establish the Lutheran church, but he translated the Bible into German, and wrote thirty-seven hymns in the vernacular for his congregation to sing. This is his best known chorale, which has been used by Bach in a cantata of the same name, by Mendelssohn in his Reformation Symphony, and by Meyerbeer in his opera, *Les Huguenots*.

All Glory, Laud and Honor

Theodulph of Orleans, a great pastor, bishop, and poet, was asked by Charlemagne to establish schools and to teach Christianity to the conquered people. To reward him for his poetic genius Charlemagne also appointed Theodulph bishop of Orleans. After Charlemagne's death, his son Louis had Theodulph imprisoned thinking he was involved in a plot against him. While imprisoned, Theodulph wrote many hymns which John Mason Neale translated from Latin to English. Melchoir Teschner, a Lutheran pastor and preacher, composed the dignified tune for which he is primarily known. A poetical rendering of Christ's triumphant entry into Jerusalem, the hymn is especially appropriate for Palm Sunday. A legend that is associated with this hymn states that Emperor Louis heard Theodulph sing from his prison cell on Palm Sunday. The emperor was so moved that he pardoned Theodulph and sent him back to his church. Truth is, however, that Theodulph died in prison.

For the Beauty of the Earth

Based on the text from James, "Every good gift and every perfect gift is from above," this is one of the most thankful of all hymns. Often used as a processional today, Pierpoint wrote it originally for use in a Communion service. He included as many sources of joy as possible in the hymn: nature,

the human family, God, and the Church. The composer of the tune, Conrad Kocher, was a student of the works of Palestrina, and was largely responsible for the reform of church music in Germany.

Sing Praise to God Who Reigns Above

John Jacob Schutz, a sometime lawyer, became a Separatist and discontinued attending Lutheran services. Schutz based this hymn on Deuteronomy 32:3—"Because I will publish the name of the Lord: ascribe ye greatness unto our God." The tune, "Mit Freuden Zart" ("With Joyful Tenderness"), is based on a pre-Reformation melody of the type that Martin Luther might have used. It was found in the Bohemian Brethren's *Kirchengesänge* of 1566.

Glorious Things of Thee Are Spoken

John Newton wrote this hymn which can be found in Book I of the *Olney Hymns,* the book of revival hymns compiled by Newton and Cowper as an instruction book in their faith. The hymn has the same first line as Psalm 87. The dignity of the words which tell of the secure place God will supply for the redeemed, are highlighted by Haydn's tune, "Austria," the tune of Austria's national hymn. The tune, written for Kaiser Franz's birthday, was apparently adapted by Haydn from a folk song. The same theme is used in the second movement of Haydn's "Emperor" String Quartet.

Praise to the Lord

Joachim Neander was one of Germany's finest hymnists and a true musician. Nineteen of his sixty hymns are set to his own melodies. In this magnificent hymn the word, "praise," begins each stanza. The tune is from Cruger's *Praxis Pietatis Melica*, called "Lobe den Herrn" ("Praise to the Lord"). It is a melody greatly loved by Germans who sang it in 1871 at a celebration of their victory over France.

The Spacious Firmament on High

Joseph Addison was an outstanding figure in eighteenth century literature. He is best known for the newspaper written with Richard Steele, *The Spectator*. In 1712 *The Spectator* published four hymns, among them this one which followed an essay called "The Strengthening of Faith." Franz Joseph Haydn composed the melody. It is an adaptation of a majestic chorus, "The Heavens Are Telling," from Haydn's oratorio, *Creation*.

O Worship the King

Sir Robert Grant who was born in India, and who became the director of the East India Company and later the Governor of Bombay, wrote this hymn. The tune, "Lyons," was composed by Johann Michael Haydn, the younger brother of Franz Joseph. As a boy he was a fine vocal soloist at St. Stephens in Vienna. Self-taught in music, Michael Haydn obtained a post at Salzburg where he taught many famous musicians such as Carl Maria von Weber. Franz Joseph thought that Michael's sacred compositions were better than his own. Michael wrote over 300 pieces for church, some of which have been mistakenly ascribed on occasion to his brother.

Joyful, Joyful, We Adore Thee

The Reverend Henry van Dyke was a Presbyterian minister who loved nature. He was an outstanding poet who used his talents to write hymns. At one point in his illustrious career he served as a preacher at Williams College. While there he wrote a hymn text to Beethoven's "Ode to Joy." What resulted was a joyously exultant nature hymn which makes a spiritual processional. Beethoven's "Ode to

Joy" is from the last movement of his *Ninth Symphony*, in which a chorus and vocal soloists are added to the orchestra to provide a thrillingly emotional climax.

Holy God, We Praise Thy Name

This hymn was taken from a poem, "Evening," which appeared in a collection called *Christian Year*, compiled by Reverend John Keble. Keble is remembered for his collection of poems for each Sunday of the year, plus other holidays and events such as Communion and Baptism. The tune is from a 1775 collection of the Austrian Empress Maria Theresa called *Katholisches Gesangbuch*.

We Gather Together

Probably, both the hymn and the tune are of folk origin. The birthplace was probably Holland which in the seventeenth century had gone through a political and religious struggle with Spain and the Catholic Church. The references in the hymn to "the wicked oppressors" and "the fight we were winning" are perhaps allusions to this historical struggle. In America this is a traditional Thanksgiving hymn.

Fairest Lord Jesus

No one knows who translated this anonymous hymn from German to English. Although some people believe it was sung about 300 years ago by German pilgrims on their way to Jerusalem (hence the name "Crusader's Hymn"), most sources of information merely state that the poem and the tune were written down in the district of Glanz from oral tradition.

Ah, Holy Jesus

This great Lutheran hymn is used during Lent. Johann Crüger composed the music and Johann Heermann wrote the words which were translated by Robert Bridges. It is a tribute to Heermann that at a time when his people were suffering through the Thirty Years War he could write, "Who was guilty. . . . 'Twas I Lord Jesus. . . . I crucified Thee." The composer, Crüger, was one of the foremost musicians of his time whose reputation rests chiefly on his excellent chorales. He was also the editor and contributor to the *Praxis Pietatis Melica*, the most important work in its field in the seventeenth century.

O Come and Mourn

This hymn was published in Frederick Faber's *Jesus and Mary* as a longer poem. It originally had twelve stanzas with the refrain, "Jesus our love is crucified," coming after each. The text is based on the Stabat Mater. Faber followed the Catholic custom of embellishing the crucifixion with a great deal of sentiment. The tune used in this book is German, being harmonized in chorale style.

O Sacred Head Now Wounded

This fourteenth century Latin hymn which is ascribed to a monk, Bernard of Clairvaux, reveals some basic medieval monastic concepts. It was thought in this period that the spirit profited from contemplation and suffering (hence the myriad of poems and art works vividly portraying the Saviour's agonies.) The monks used to have crucifixes in their cells upon which they concentrated intently each day. Therefore, in this hymn the writer speaks of seven parts of Jesus' body: His feet, knees, hands, side, breast, heart, and head. The melody of the hymn was originally a German love song, "Mein G'müth ist mir verwirret" (Confused Is My Heart). It was not uncommon at that time to place religious words to secular tunes. The tune was composed by Hans Leo Hassler, who was greatly influenced by Italian music, having studied in Venice as a young man. Hassler was an organist to the Electoral Chapel at Dresden, and a Renaissance composer of high repute.

Joy Dawned Again On Easter Day

The authorship of this hymn is uncertain. It is from the third part of an ancient Latin hymn sometimes ascribed to Ambrose, but it has not been specifically mentioned as such by early historians. John Mason Neale translated the hymn from Latin. The tune "Lasst uns erfreuen" (Let Us Rejoice) comes from a Cologne collection of hymns of 1623, Geistliche Kirchengesäng (Spiritual Church Songs).

Now Thank We All Our God

Martin Rinkart was a bishop in Eilenberg, Germany, during the Thirty Years War. In 1637 when thousands of people died in a pestilence, he conducted forty to fifty funerals a day. Nonetheless, he found time to write sixty-six hymns. This hymn, a triumph of the spirit over pestilence and war's misfortunes, is all the more amazing since Rinkart's own condition was so desperate, and his debts exceeded his income for several years in the future. The melody, written by Johann Crüger, was later used by Bach as the basis for a cantata.

Jesu, Joy of Man's Desiring

Bach used this chorale as the sixth and last movements in his Cantata 147, "Herz und Mund und That und Leben" ("Heart and Mouth and Deeds and Life"). The original melody was by Johann Schop, composer, violinist, lutenist, and trombonist in Hamburg, Germany in the early seventeenth century. The text was written by Martin Janus. In the Bach arrangement, the four-part chorale is juxtaposed with a beautiful running contrapuntal accompaniment.

Jesus, Priceless Treasure

This hymn, with words by Johann Franck, was first set to music by Johann Crüger, who wrote the outstanding hymnal of the seventeenth century, *Praxis Pietatis Melica.* As cantor of the Saint Nicholas Church, he wrote many strong tunes for his congregation. Under the German title *Jesu Meine Freude,* this first appeared in the 1653 edition of *Praxis.* A favorite melody, Bach used it in Cantatas 64, 81, and 87. His third motet called *Jesu Meine Freude,* is based entirely on this chorale.

Come Blessed Death

Bach contributed sixty-nine harmonizations of sacred songs to a song book compiled in Leipzig in 1736 by Georg Christian Schemelli. Many of the songs had the characteristics of a chorale. Others were of a freer nature, and can be described as arias or sacred songs. This is one of the loveliest, most expressive melodies from the collection.

Wake, Awake, For Night Is Flying

Pastor Phillip Nicolai composed this, one of the greatest German hymns, in 1597 in the midst of a bubonic plague, which killed 1,300 people in six months. Bach composed a cantata (No. 140) of the same name based on this chorale.

O Saviour, Hear Me

This setting is an adaptation of an extract from Christoph Gluck's most famous opera, *Orpheus and Eurydice.* Gluck, an operatic reformer, preferred classical subjects, but felt that the music should be secondary to the drama and poetry. "Orpheus" is the earliest full-length opera by any composer in the repertoires of most opera companies today.

Jesu, Word of God Incarnate

The poignant *Ave Verum* text has been a favorite with sacred music composers of all centuries. Mozart composed this motet in June, 1791 at Baden, Germany. This setting scored originally for soprano, alto, tenor, and bass voices, with string quartet accompaniment. However, organ or piano accompaniment is most often heard today.

Ave Maria

The "Ave Maria" is one of the great Catholic prayers that has received many choral settings by composers of all periods. Schubert set seven songs to Sir Walter Scott's poem, "The Lady of the Lake." The "Ave Maria" was the sixth setting, and is a good example of Schubert's great gift for wedding poetry with appropriately expressive melodies. In a letter Schubert commented to his father and stepmother about this song: "I never force myself to be devout, except when I feel so inspired, and never compose hymns or prayers unless I feel within me real and true devotion." This etherial melody moves within a small range of seven notes in contrast to the wide arpeggios in the original accompaniment.

But the Lord Is Mindful of His Own

This solo from Felix Mendelssohn's oratorio, *Saint Paul,* is the only selection from the work that receives regular performances today. The oratorio tells of Saint Paul, who before being converted to Christianity, witnessed the stoning of Saint Stephen, the first Christian martyr, outside of Jerusalem sometime after the crucifixion.

O Rest in the Lord

This piece occurs as selection thirty-one in Mendelssohn's *Elijah,* and is one of the most widely known oratorio solos. Mendelssohn, however, did not like the song and felt that it should be omitted from the oratorio because the tune was too sweet and reminiscent of the Scottish ballad. However, under pressure from his friends, he altered a few notes, and the tune remains.

Cast Thy Burden Upon the Lord

This chorale, a quartet from Mendelssohn's oratorio, *Elijah*, where it appears as the fifteenth selection, was originally meant to be accompanied by violin. *Elijah*, the most popular oratorio since Handel's time, was first performed in Birmingham, England, in 1846 with Mendelssohn conducting. The story tells of the prophet Elijah, who influenced the children of Israel to worship Jehovah God instead of idols.

Children's Prayer
from "Hansel and Gretel"

The German composer, Humperdinck, wrote five operas, but none of his others were as successful as *Hansel and Gretel* in which this duet occurs. First produced in Weimar, Germany, in 1893, *Hansel and Gretel* was also welcomed by audiences in London and New York. People enjoyed the fresh subject as well as the melodic beauty of the score.

Come, Thou Almighty King

One of the most popular Holy Trinity hymns, this hymn has been translated into many languages. The name of the author is unknown but he is thought to have lived at the same time as the Wesleys. The hymn was originally written to be sung to the tune of the British national anthem, "God Save the King." Revolutionary War history states that one Sunday, during the Revolutionary War, British troops invaded a church on Long Island, New York and ordered the congregation to stand and sing "God Save the King." The people obliged by singing the requested tune but with the hymn text "Come, Thou Almighty King"! Now the "Italian Hymn" or "Trinity" by Felice de Giardini is used as the tune. Giardini, an Italian violinist, was a prolific composer of operas, violin music, quartets, sonatas, and concertos. This tune was one of several contributed by Giardini to a London collection of psalms and hymns.

The Strife Is O'er

This Latin hymn of unknown origin is one of the most well-known resurrection hymns. It first appeared in a hymn collection in 1695, from which it was translated by Francis Pott. The tune is a response by the composer Giovanni Pierluigi da Palestrina, one of the musical giants of the sixteenth century which is often called "The Golden Age of Choral Music."

Lord, Dismiss Us With Thy Blessing

For a long time the author of this hymn was unknown. It was probably difficult to trace because there are four hymns that have this same first line. The most authoritative source on hymnology, John Julian, states in his dictionary that Reverend John Fawcett probably wrote these words. The tune, "Sicilian Mariner's Hymn," of unknown origin, is the same tune for the Christmas carol "O Sanctissima."

All People That On Earth Do Dwell

Although there used to be controversy over the authorship of this hymn, scholars now agree that it was written by the Puritan, William Kethe, a native of Scotland who moved to Geneva to escape the wrath of Queen Mary. There Kethe translated the scriptures into the Geneva Bible, which was brought to America on the Mayflower. He also helped with the Anglo-Genevan Psalter, compiled in Geneva. Twenty-five of his metrical renderings of psalms appear in both that book and

The Sternhold and Hopkins Psalter, a later compilation of metrical Psalms. The tune known as "Old Hundred" by Louis Bourgeois, is the same tune used for "The Doxology." Originally the tempo was spritely. Such tunes were called "Geneva jiggs" by Queen Elizabeth I.

O Sons and Daughters

No information is available about the author of this hymn, Jean Tisserand, other than that he was a friar of French nationality who died in 1494. The hymn, used in many French dioceses on the evening of Easter Day, is definitely a joyous Easter carol. The melody dates from the fifteenth century.

Doxology

A bishop, Thomas Ken, wrote this hymn in 1709. The most popular hymn to the Trinity in America, it has been used for sacred occasions in church and public life: worship, baptisms, funerals, dedications, and at the end of a war. When Ken, a highly principled man refused to read *The King's Declaration of Indulgence* from the pulpit, he was imprisoned. Louis Bourgeois who composed the tune also endured prison; he had harmonized several hymn melodies against the command of Calvin, who believed hymns should be sung in unison or not at all.

O What Their Joy and Their Glory Must Be

Peter Abelard, a brilliant medieval scholar and teacher attracted pupils from many lands. After a love affair with disastrous personal consequences, Peter became a monk and forced Heloise, his lady, to become a nun. Abelard wrote for her a complete hymnal to cover the important days of the liturgy. Although all of Abelard's hymns are preserved in a Brussels manuscript, this one and a hymn about the crucifixion are the only ones widely used today.

O Gladsome Light

Sometimes called "A Hymn for the Lighting of the Lamps," this hymn probably dates from the third century. It is a Greek hymn translated by Robert Bridges. Early Christians connected religion with nature by the use of metaphors. In this hymn, daylight, sunset, and night are compared by the poet to the Trinity. The melody used in this book is attributed to Louis Bourgeois.

Turn Back, O Man

Clifford Bax, who gave up the study of art for literature, won great distinction for his plays in which music played a significant part. This poem was written after World War I and urges men to rethink their attitudes toward both war and religion. The tune used here is by Louis Bourgeois. Gustav Holst is one of the major composers who found inspiration for anthems in this hymn.

Praise Ye the Lord of Hosts

Camille Saint-Saëns' *Christmas Oratorio* was composed in the author's youth. This charming work for strings, harp, and organ was completed in just twelve days and given to his choristers at the Madelaine Cathedral on December 15, 1858. The work is divided into nine numbers, based on texts from the Office of the Day and the Midnight Mass. It has become a perennial favorite among church choirs.

The Palms

Jean Baptiste Fauré, the composer of this song, was a prize-winning French singer with a glorious operatic voice. (He should not be confused with his more famous contemporary, Gabriel

Fauré.) "The Palms"—"Les Rameaux" in French—appears in Jean Baptiste Fauré's two-volume collection of songs and is a universal favorite for Palm Sunday.

Christ, We Do All Adore Thee

This is the final chorus from Theodore Dubois' very popular oratorio, *Les Sept Paroles de Christ* (The Seven Last Words of Christ). Dubois, a French organist and teacher, won the Prix de Rome while studying at the Paris Conservatoire. In 1866 he was choirmaster and organist at St. Clothilde, where this oratorio was first performed. Later on he became organist at the Madelaine, succeeding another French composer, Camille Saint-Saëns.

O Lord Most Holy

Cësar Franck wrote this in 1872 for tenor soloist, organ, harp, cello, and double bass, and it has been interpolated into his *Mass For Three Solo Voices* which was written earlier. The text is from St. Thomas Aquinas' communion hymn of the same name. The Latin title, *Panis Angelicas*, means "Bread of Angels." In the original version the composer ingeniously arranged the melody into a canon, which gives the effect of a musical echo, and subtle harmonies lend a mystic quality.

Gentle Jesus

This song was originally intended to be performed as a boy soprano solo in Gabriel Fauré's *Requiem*. Today a female soprano usually sings the solo. The *Requiem* is Fauré's most performed major work. He composed it in 1886 while he was choirmaster at the Church of the Madelaine in Paris. For a long time Fauré was not recognized as a great composer, but in the twentieth century he received acclaim as an innovator of French contemporary music. The *Requiem* was com-

posed in honor of his father, and was originally scored for a very small orchestra of solo violin, violas, cellos, basses, harp, three trombones, and an organ. The symphonic version was made thirteen years later in 1899.

Be Still, My Soul

The author of this hymn was the head of the Women's House of the Evangelical Lutheran Church in Germany. The hymn, discovered and translated by Jane L. Borthwick, might have been based on Psalm 46: "Be still and know that I am God." The popularity of the hymn today is largely due to Jan Sibelius' *Finlandia*, the tune to which the hymn text is sung. Sibelius' strong Finnish personality caused him to be regarded as the model for Finnish nationalism in music.

God the Omnipotent

This hymn is a composite of Henry Chorley's "In Time of War" and Canon John Ellerton's "God the Almighty One." Chorley was a music critic and writer in London, and Ellerton was a curate and respected hymnologist in Brighton, England. Stanzas three through five of this hymn were taken from another Ellerton hymn written four days before a battle in the Franco-Prussian War of 1870. Although England was not fighting, the people were concerned because only the Channel separated them from the war. The "Russian Hymn" tune, written by Alexis F. Lvov in answer to a request by Emperor Nicholas, has also been used by Tchaikovsky in his *Overture 1812*.

Now On Land and Sea Descending

Samuel Longfellow, the brother of the famous American poet, was, himself, a rather good poet. While pastor of a Unitarian Church in Brooklyn, New York, he inaugurated vesper services and, in 1859 prepared a book of vespers from which this hymn comes. In addition, he also compiled two hymnals, a book of poetry, and wrote a biography of his brother. The composer of the "Vesper Hymn," Dimitri Bortniansky, a protégé of the Russian empress Catherine, and who became choirmaster of the Imperial Chapel, systematized Russian sacred music and has been called the father of Russian church music.

Praise to the Living God

The "Yigdal," a Hebrew song of praise from the twelfth century, is a Jewish doxology still heard in synagogues today. It is based on the Thirteen Articles of Faith as drawn up by Moses Maimonides (1130-1205), a Hebrew scholar who formulated the Dogmas of Judaism. The "Yigdal" is in the daily prayer service, and is sung at the conclusion of the service on Sabbath eves and festivals.

Rock of Ages

This old synagogal melody is the best known melody for the joyous festival of Hanukkah, the December holiday celebrating the Maccabean military victory for religious freedom. The holiday lasts for eight days, because after the victory an eight-branched candlestick, the menorah, was lit in the Temple of Jerusalem. Although there was but a small amount of oil, miraculously the menorah burned for eight days.

Title Index

Index of First Lines

Index of Sources